EUROPA ⚔ MILITARIA
SPECIAL Nº5

WELLINGTON'S ARMY

RECREATED IN

COLOUR PHOTOGRAPHS

NEIL LEONARD

Windrow & Greene

© 1994 Windrow & Greene Ltd.
Printed in Singapore

This edition published
in Great Britain 1994 by
Windrow & Greene Ltd.
19a Floral Street
London WC2E 9DS

Designed by John Anastasio/Creative Line

A CIP catalogue record for this book is available
from the British Library.

ISBN 1 872004 79 2

Acknowledgements:
The author would like to express grateful thanks to
his friends and colleagues in the world of Napoleonic
re-enactment - too numerous to mention - for their
patience and kind assistance over the past year and
more, during the assembly of the photographs which
make up this book. Especial thanks to historian and
author Stuart Reid for his assistance and advice
throughout; to Philip Elliott-Wright, historian,
author, and for many years Secretary of the
Napoleonic Association, for his kindness in contributing
the Introduction; and to my long-suffering wife for her
patience, and tolerance of this sometimes all-consuming hobby.

Contact addresses: Readers wishing to find out more
about Napoleonic re-enactment in the UK, France and
Germany, or about the groups and societies featured
in this book, may contact them through the author:
Neil Leonard, Rose Cottage, Caledonia, Winlanton,
Tyne & Wear NE21 6AX – who may also be contacted
for enquiries regarding the recently formed
European Napoleonic Federation.The Napoleonic Association
may be contacted through the Secretary: Adrian Proudfoot,
3 Steadman Avenue, Cosby, Leicester LE9 5UZ. Some
individual group contact addresses are listed in the
1994 edition of Windrow & Greene's Militaria Directory
& Sourcebook (ISBN I 872004 84 9: £14.95) available
through bookshops or direct from the publisher.

The Napoleonic Association

The re-creation of historic battles for commemorative purposes has a long history: there are accounts of the ancient Egyptians, Greeks and Romans re-enacting military victories for mass public entertainments. In 1687 King James II of England had the siege of Budapest re-enacted for the public on Hounslow Heath to mark the participation in the battle of his natural son the Duke of Berwick. During the Napoleonic Wars both Regular and Militia units frequently staged battle displays in Hyde Park for the entertainment and reassurance of the public. The military "tattoo", often involving symbolic re-enactment of a famous victory, has been a continuing tradition in many countries during the 19th and 20th centuries. All these, however, have been state or regimental events; re-creations by groups of private individuals are relatively recent phenomena.

These private revivals of an ancient tradition had their origins in the 1960s when, in both Britain and the United States, a mixture of civilians and military personnel sharing a fascination with military history came together in groups dedicated to re-enacting particular periods. On both sides of the Atlantic the first groups began by re-enacting their respective Civil Wars. In Britain the late Brigadier Peter Young led the way with the foundation in 1968 of the Sealed Knot; and by the early 1970s other groups were forming to re-create subjects ranging from Roman legionaries and medieval knights to Napoleonic soldiers.

It was in 1970 that a number of like-minded individuals inspired by the example of the Sealed Knot set out to form a Napoleonic re-enactment group; this Sabre Society brought together enthusiasts from all over the British Isles. By 1973 the society had several hundred members in both British "redcoat" and French Imperial regiments; and its early success was marked by its appearance in the week-long Regency celebrations held that year in Lichfield. Many of the townspeople dressed up in period costume and laid on various contemporary scenarios; and large numbers from the Sabre Society not only staged the now-familiar battle re-enactments but also helped bring the period to life by taking part in "street theatre". This belief that the whole gamut of period life should be re-created, and not only the military elements, has remained an integral part of Napoleonic re-enactment ever since.

In 1975, due to internal disagreements, the Sabre Society divided. A group of twelve members (including Howard Giles and myself) set up the Napoleonic Association, dedicated not only to re-creating the period in its widest sense, but also to stimulating original historical research. Hence, from the beginning, the Association has had two parallel elements: the battle re-enactment and "living history" section, and the research section. The motivation which drives individuals to join a re-enactment group often fuels an ambition to reproduce the minutiae of their chosen period as closely as is possible in the late 20th century. The re-enactors and researchers draw inspiration from each other: the progress of research provides a continuous flow of information which enables the re-enactors' uniforms, equipment and re-creations to reflect the most recent and detailed knowledge of the period; and re-enactments provide, in turn, both a focus and a ready source of enthusiasts for the research.

Today the Napoleonic Association has over 400 members in Great Britain and has gained a reputation for accuracy, authenticity and attention to detail. Re-created British units include, among others, the Highlanders of the 42nd Regiment (The Black Watch), the 45th (Nottinghamshire) Regiment, and the green-clad 95th Rifles. Surprisingly to some, Napoleon himself can still inspire the modern

student of history to the extent that the Association also boasts French units, the largest being the 21st Line Infantry. The Association's oldest formation is the Austrian Infantry Regiment No.4 "Hoch und Deutsch meister". Cavalry and artillery are fielded at all large events, including such mounted units as the 1st Life Guards, the 12th Light Dragoons and the 15th Hussars.

Over the past twenty-odd years each summer has seen the various elements of the Association and other groups joining together to stage re-creations of the period - ranging from full-scale actions, through skirmishes and military camps, to civilian balls - right across England, before audiences of thousands.

Members also regularly link up with Napoleonic enthusiasts in France, Germany, Belgium and the Czech Republic to take part in spectacular battles involving several thousand participants. The 175th anniversary of Waterloo in 1990 saw over 2,000 people from across Europe and even from North America gather on the field of battle in Belgium to stage a re-enactment before an audience estimated at 50,000. Similar multi-national gatherings have seen battles re-enacted at Jena, Leipzig, Austerlitz, and Borodino. Members of the Association have also worked with the BBC on the television documentary series *Soldiers*; and have even taken part in a "musical battle" accompanied by the bands of the Grenadier and Irish Guards. With numerous bi-centennial events planned over the next twenty-one years, the Association aims to remain at the forefront of Napoleonic re-enactment both in Britain and in Continental Europe.

Philip J.C.Elliott-Wright

(**Above**) One of barely a dozen original 1799 pattern Line infantry rankers' jackets known to survive, from the hundreds of thousands made. This Battalion company jacket of the 26th Regiment (Cameronians) is today in the Musee de l'Emperi at Salon de Provence, France, and displays all the conventional features. Of a coarse, heavy woollen broadcloth with a felted surface, coats were dyed red with madder; the colour faded and dulled in use. Regiments had distinctive coloured facings on the collar, cuffs and shoulder straps; even though all Guards and "Royal"-titled regiments were faced dark blue, there were obviously not enough colours available for the 100-odd units to have individual facings. Regiments were further distinguished by the design and placing of the "lace" - the worsted tape - sewn to the faced areas, skirt turnbacks, and to the front and rear in buttonhole "loops". Battalion companies - i.e. all except the Grenadier and Light Infantry "flank" companies in each battalion - wore a tuft of worsted fringing at the base of the shoulder straps. The 1st Bn., 26th Foot fought in the Peninsula.

(**Right**) The research side of re--enactment can be very interesting, and it is unfortunate that relatively few people pursue it. Those coming into the hobby will normally either be loaned the necessary equipment, or buy it from established suppliers. They thus miss out on the pleasure and satisfaction of original detective work. Primary research in the archives of Britain's many small, often neglected regimental museums can pay dividends. This photo shows a find in the Northumberland Fusiliers Museum, where a small package hidden among a pile of catalogued boxes yielded a sealed pattern of facing cloth; though dating from the 1830s it gives a clue to the type of material used for uniforms - a heavy wool which could be cut and left with raw unhemmed edges without fraying. Suitable cloth for making reconstruction uniforms is today hard to come by; but it has been made for centuries by A.W.Hainsworth & Sons of Pudsey near Leeds, who still supply British Army ceremonial costume. Various period sources list the facings of the old 5th Foot as "gosling green" or "olive drab".

4

5ᵗʰ Foot.

6/3/35 Lieut F.R. Pyner
facings of coatee by Messʳˢ Coles
to this shade, being sealed pattern
of the Colonel as per Captᵗ Spencer
on 25/10/33.

"Gosling Green"

This shade constant
to Mᵉ Gones

(**Above left**) Battalion company soldier's jacket of the 83rd Reg-iment, now in the Musee de l'Armee, Paris; the 2nd Bn. of the 83rd served in the Peninsula. Surviving jacket buttons are of flat pewter, bearing the regiment's number alone or within a border. There were normally ten front "loops", set singly or, as here, in spaced pairs, supposedly horizontal but sometimes, again as here, slanted; cuffs and false pocket flaps bore four loops each, though one is now missing from each cuff here. Regimental identifying features were the patterns of coloured lines woven into the tape - for the 83rd, one red and one green stripe, green innermost; and the shaping of the loops. The 83rd had square outer ends; other shapes were pointed, or "Jew's harp" or "flowerpot" variations of the three-pointed "bastion" shape. Jackets were supplied to the units from various contractors, unfitted and sometimes imperfectly finished; surviving examples often seem to be unissued coats, and minor variations are common.

(**Above right**) Shoulder of the jacket of a drummer boy of the Northumberland Militia, c.1810. It is important evidence for the method of making the shoulder "wings" also added to the jackets of the Grenadier and Light companies within each infantry battalion - a feature that many reconstructors today tend to get horribly wrong. As with all issued items, standards would have varied with dispersed manufacture by sometimes rascally contractors, but this is a fine example. The wings were made from two layers of cloth and padded with scraps or tailors' offcuttings. The tufted wool fringing was made from drawn strands much in the manner of a pompon; it seems normally to have been plain white, this fancy tricolour effect possibly being limited to the unit's drummers. However, there are examples of multi-coloured tufts even on Battalion company shoulder straps - see the 26th jacket opposite.

(**Top left**) The burnished brass bayonet crossbelt plate for a private in the re-created 1st Regiment of Foot, the Royal Scots. This copy was made from an original held in the collection of the United Services Museum in Edinburgh Castle. The plate was immersed in silicone rubber solution, leaving a perfect mould from which brass copies could be cast using the lost wax method.

(**Left & above right**) The minor details shown here - the embroidered tail of an officer's shabraque, and the rear of the cuff of an officer's pelisse, from items held in the collection of the 15th/19th Hussars Museum - may not seem important to the casual observer. However, when this level of detail is incorporated into a well-made reproduction it produces an accurate and pleasing impression. Comparison with similar reproductions made without the same degree of attention to detail will immediately show that it makes all the difference.

(**Right**) The backbone of Wellington's infantry - the long-service sergeant, of which each company had two. This sergeant of the re-created 68th (Durham) Light Infantry wears the home service uniform, also worn on campaign before 1809: the shako, tight leather neck stock, red jacket, white breeches, and knee-length black cloth gaiters. The 1806 pattern felt shako bears a black cockade and a regimental button, the green worsted tuft of the Light Infantry, and one of the buglehorn badges which replaced the brass plate of Line troops in Light units. Sergeants' jackets were of finer scarlet cloth than those of the "private centinells"; this one bears the fringed wings which distinguished Light Infantry regiments and companies, who also displayed sergeants' chevrons of rank on both sleeves rather than the right only. Sleeve chevrons had replaced epaulettes and shoulder knots in 1802; for sergeants they were of plain white lace on a backing of facing colour. Sergeants were also identified by a crimson worsted waist sash with a central stripe of regimental facing colour.

Wellington's Army

Among military history enthusiasts at every level the British Army of the Napoleonic period enjoys enduring popularity as a subject of study. There seem to be several linked reasons for the special aura surrounding the memory of that long-suffering, hard-marching, hard-fighting, hard-bitten little army (for it *was* small - in the field, much smaller than the British contingent in the Gulf War of 1991).

One certain reason is that the British Army began the nearly twenty years of the Napoleonic Wars generally despised for its professional ineptitude; and fought its way through a score of battles to earn the respect of the whole military world. The appeal of the underdog who comes from behind to win, and win again, is irresistible. In the early 1790s the British Army had sunk into the habits of incompetence and defeat; by 1815 it had acquired the habits of efficiency and victory.

An important element in the army's transformation was the happy chance that from 1808 to 1815 its most important active field force was commanded by a man of outstanding talent and character: Arthur Wellesley, First Duke of Wellington, and arguably Britain's greatest soldier. Other commanders of skill and vision played important roles in improving the army's competence and confidence - notably, Sir John Moore; but Wellington's leading contribution is undeniable. He was the general who understood it; who schooled it, shaped it, bullied it and cursed it; cared for it, argued and laboured for it tirelessly, year after thankless year. He was also a field commander of near-genius, who led it in a procession of victories until the terrible night of Waterloo fell at last over the final battlefield.

This was also the first British expeditionary army which has left us fairly full and accessible documentary records. We can understand, more or less, how it was organised and how it worked; and this pattern is satisfyingly recognisable to our detective instincts. It shows, in "ancestral" terms at least, the basic features of Britain's later armies.

The tactics this army and its opponents employed in battle are easy to follow: we can see how and why particular actions were won and lost. Some British students may also find a special appeal in the traditionally defensive tactics which won it so many of its battles: the thin red line, drawn up on carefully chosen ground, standing like a wall in the face of repeated enemy assaults. (There is a legend that one French general left the field of Waterloo lamenting, "It has always been the same, ever since Crecy...").

The written record also includes, again for the first time, a mass of private memoirs - and not only those of officers. Before 1800 authentic voices from the ranks are few; but from Wellington's army we have a number of lively personal accounts, giving a sharply drawn individual face and character to the previously anonymous redcoat. That most of these soldiers are revealed as impressively tough, brave, fair-minded men only adds to the appeal of the period. Their regiments, too, are often given distinctive characters and traditions in these memoirs, adding another dimension of interest to campaign history.

All in all, then, the lasting glamour of Wellington's army is understandable. It was an army at the peak of its powers; made up of impressive individuals, attractively recognisable to modern British readers; led by an inspired commander, whose colourful character is recorded in dozens of anecdotes; winning battles, at odds, against the armies of one of history's greatest conquerors; and finally victorious in a great world war. Its leader called it "...the most complete machine for its numbers now existing in Europe...I could have done anything with that army. It was in such perfect order."

And finally, of course, there were the uniforms...

Martin Windrow

Taking The King's Shilling

At the outbreak of the Napoleonic Wars the common soldier was generally regarded with contempt by his fellow countrymen. The regular army offered a wretched life for an unlimited period of service, and voluntary enlistment was believed to attract only desperate characters. Recruiters attended magistrates' courts, seeking to fill the ranks with debtors, vagabonds and petty criminals who were allowed to "take the King's shilling" as the alternative to transportation to penal colonies.

The civil population usually met the redcoat under hostile circumstances. Before 1792 there were few purpose-built barracks in England; troops were billeted in public houses, farms and private property designated by local Watch Committees, their unwilling hosts obliged to provide quarters, food and candles. Soldiers were therefore an unwelcome sight, considered as the off-scourings of society: in Wellington's own much-quoted phrase, "the scum of the earth, enlisted for drink".

Even in wartime the army never resorted to conscription (unlike the Royal Navy); so somehow, recruits had to be attracted, as the ranks were thinned by Peninsula casualties and the ravages of disease in unhealthy colonies such as the West Indies.

Some reforms were introduced in the early 1800s to make service more attractive: these included limited-length enlistments (often of three successive periods of seven years), and pensions. As the war progressed and victories raised the army's reputation, many decent men were drawn to the army by patriotism or an adventurous spirit. Battalions authorised to "beat up" a locality (i.e. to rouse it with beating drums) would send out recruiting parties of an officer, two sergeants, a drummer and a few men. Dressed in specially smartened uniforms, with bunches of ribbons in their caps, they would spread out across the countryside in search of prey, often supported by posters claiming that their own particularly famous and distinguished corps had room for a few of the very best men...

The recruiters would prowl country fairs, alehouses and market places, turning the heads of likely young men with the dash of the smart red jacket, the stirring beat of the drum, bantering challenges to their pride, outrageous lies about army life - and large quantities of free ale.... They promised large bounties for enlistment; but did not explain that paying for celebratory drinks, and a compulsory charge "for his knapsack", would leave the hapless recruit little to show for it when morning dawned.

One source of desirable recruits was the Militia, a nationwide part-time force raised - for home defence service only - by compulsory ballot, and uniformed and equipped much like the Line, for which it provided a large pool of trained soldiers. Recruiting parties from the Line were permitted to address paraded Militia units, offering volunteers a large bounty and the chance to play their part in heroic deeds overseas. Many Militia soldiers did volunteer to transfer; some liked what they had seen of the military life, some hankered for adventure, some were lured by the bounty (at up to 12 guineas, this could equal many months' pay), and some had a pressing need to travel due to romantic complications.

(Above) A smart young sergeant of the Light Infantry company of the 1st Regiment of Foot, the Royal Scots, in post-1812 uniform. Such a famous and ancient corps as "Pontius Pilate's Bodyguard" would offer plenty of scope for the recruiting sergeant's boasts and promises as he dazzled the yokels outside the village inns: tales of glory, fiery Spanish senoritas, and French gold littering the battlefields just waiting to be scooped up.

(Left) The drummer was an essential member of the recruiting party, his stirring rolls and ruffles always gathering a crowd: "drumming and fifing were heard in the streets from dawn until dusk". Drummers' uniforms were traditionally decorated with extra lace and shoulder wings. This is a reconstruction of a drummer of the 1st Foot Guards, 1812-1815; such an elite regiment could choose its recruits with some care.

The Infantry

The red-coated footsoldier is the most enduring image of Wellington's army. He was the backbone upon whom the outcome of every battle depended; cavalry and artillery could affect a battle, but the stoic defiance of infantry in defence, or their aggression in the assault, nearly always decided the day. On the battlefields of Spain and Portugal the redcoats of the Peninsular field army reached their pinnacle of achievement, earning world-wide respect for their steadiness, discipline, and coolness under fire - a reputation immortalised at Waterloo.

Given that his pay was only a shilling a day (actually reduced by "stoppages" to a handful of coppers a week); that discipline was enforced by the threat of the lash; and that campaign life for the Napoleonic footsoldier could be savagely hard, the redcoat's record was astonishing. Yet rankers' memoirs prove that they were anything but cowed slave-soldiers, but rather volunteer professionals who took pride in their service and their regiments.

There were, at most, 104 numbered infantry regiments, some raised during the war and fairly short-lived. Most had a territorial title as well, but recruiting was not limited to these counties; and many Irishmen served in nominally English and Scottish regiments. Some regiments had one, some two, a few three or even four battalions, giving a total in 1809 of 179 battalions. The battalion was the tactical unit, three or four being gathered into a brigade; battalions of the same regiment seldom served together. The British Army was stretched over many fronts; in 1809 there were 26 red-coated British battalions in the Peninsula, and in early 1814 about 50; there were 23 in Wellington's multi-national army at Waterloo in 1815.

The battalion was organised in ten companies: one Grenadier (in theory, the tallest, strongest men); one Light Infantry (in theory, the best shots and most agile skirmishers) - these collectively being termed the "flank companies"; and eight Battalion or Centre companies. Battalion strength was in theory around 1,000 all ranks, but on campaign this could dwindle to 500 or less. Severely weakened battalions might be amalgamated or broken up.

Apart from the green-jacketed Rifles (and units of German and Portuguese allies and mercenaries) the line of battle comprised red-coated Foot Guards, Line, Light and Highland battalions. There were minor differences of uniform and drill, but all these units were trained to perform basically the same duties and to fight in the same way with the same weapons.

(Above) "The swan doth like the water clear/ so too the hussar good ale and beer/ so come my lads, let's have no fear/ come 'list today and drink our beer". So wrote a recruiting sergeant from a hussar regiment as he plied his craft round the taprooms, market squares and village greens of the North and Midlands. His lawful prey came in many shapes and sizes. A surviving, and probably typical record lists recruits aged anything from 15 to 35 years old; 44 per cent measured 5ft.4ins. or less, and only 16 per cent more than 5ft.7ins; the great majority would have been rural labourers or poor urban tradesmen. For the most destitute the prospect of a blanket, a roof, two meals a day and a few shillings a week were enough. As for the rest, the bounty, the free drinks, and the allure of such splendid uniforms as this reconstruction of a 15th Hussars sergeant lured many types: innocent young lads, serious-minded patriots, orphans or bastards from parish poorhouses, servants tired of their masters, husbands tired of nagging wives, and unintentional fathers who had no wish to acquire them.

Once he had taken the symbolic shilling the recruit was taken before the District Surgeon for a physical examination. If passed fit (having "no Rupture, nor was ever troubled with Fits, and am no Ways disabled by Lameness or otherwise, but have the perfect use of my Limbs..."), the recruit was attested by a magistrate, signing the Articles of War. He received his bounty of perhaps 10 guineas; and, after a reasonable interval for his new comrades to relieve him of most of it, was marched off with his fellow recruits to the nearest depot.

Opposite: Reconstruction of Battalion company soldiers of the 9th Foot, the East Norfolk Regiment, in the uniform of 1812-1815.

(Left) Men of the re-created 9th Foot in the uniform of 1812-1815 and full marching order. The "stovepipe" shako was replaced beginning in 1812 by this "Belgic" model (not a contemporary term - it resembled the shako worn by Belgian troops). This had a high "false" front, a universal pattern brass plate bearing the King's cypher (with sometimes a regimental number and/or a traditional "ancient badge"), a tasselled cord festoon, and a tuft rising from a black cockade on the left side. For Battalion companies the cord was white, the tuft white over red; for Grenadiers, both white; for Light Infantry, both green.

From 1809 loose grey "pantaloon" trousers were issued for campaign dress (white ones had been worn in hot climates for some years), with short grey cloth half-gaiters; these were ordered into general use in 1811.

The cartridge pouch, holding 60 rounds, hung from one crossbelt behind the right hip. The bayonet scabbard hung on the left hip from the other crossbelt

(when "walking out" this bayonet belt, with its gleaming plate, was the only equipment worn). Slung to hang over it were the linen haversack carrying campaign rations; and the "Italian"-style three-pint water canteen.

A blanket/greatcoat roll was strapped to the Trotter knapsack. Here the pack is painted with the regimental number and a version of the 9th's Britannia badge (which led to them being nicknamed "the Virgins" in Catholic Spain); evidence is scarce, but some packs seem to have been painted with quite intricate coloured badges. The Trotter was smart, its black lacquered canvas squared off by an internal wooden box frame; but it was not a practical design. When it was full and heavy the frame chafed the back painfully, breaking the skin in bloody "pack palsy"; and the chest strap joining the shoulder straps restricted the lungs dangerously - on hard marches men died in the ranks under this burden. The Trotter knapsack would continue to plague the redcoat until 1871.

(Left) Firing the Tower musket ("Brown Bess"), in various slightly differing models the redcoat's standard weapon from the late 17th to the mid-19th century. Just under or over 5ft. long, weighing 10 to 11lbs., this muzzle-loading smooth-bore flintlock normally had a bore of .75in. and fired a 1oz. soft lead ball thrown by a charge of around 1oz. of black powder.

To load, the soldier took from his pouch a tubular folded paper cartridge, holding a measured powder charge and a ball, and bit off one end (army surgeons always checked a would-be recruit's teeth). A priming pan on the right of the breech was covered by a spring-loaded striker plate ("frizzen"); the soldier poured some of the powder into the pan, closing it with the frizzen. He then grounded the butt, poured the rest of the powder into the muzzle, and pushed ball and paper after it. He slid the steel ramrod from its pipes under the barrel, tamped down charge and ball, and returned the ramrod.

To fire, he pulled back the spring-loaded "cock" holding a wedge of flint in its jaws; aimed along the barrel; and pulled the trigger. The cock fell, the flint striking the frizzen and pushing it forward; the impact sent a shower of sparks into the now-exposed priming pan; the priming ignited, sending sparks through a touch – hole in the side of the breech to set off the main charge.

A fully trained man could load and fire twice or three times in a minute. Flintlock muskets were accurate only to 50 or 60 yards, but individual marksmanship seldom mattered: most troops fired in massed volleys against similar closely drawn-up bodies of men, and at 100 to 200 yards about half the balls might strike home.

Flintlocks had many drawbacks. The black powder quickly fouled the touch-hole, which needed frequent cleaning with a small pricker and brush. Flints often needed adjustment or replacing. Flaring priming could cause painful injury in the close-packed ranks: some men lost eyes or ears. The long "hang-fire" between the ignition of priming and main charge made marksmanship even more difficult. In rainy or even very damp weather the exposed powder failed to take fire. Finally, unless there was a brisk breeze, a few volleys quickly wrapped the ranks in a blinding cloud of impenetrable white smoke. (Photos: Time Machine Ltd.)

(Right) An off-duty man of a Battalion company of the 9th Foot. Each numbered company comprised,in theory: a captain commanding; two lieutenants or ensigns; two sergeants; three corporals; a drummer, and in some battalions a fifer - though drummers seem often to have carried both instruments; and 85 to 100 privates.

In practice these numbers would seldom be achieved, and almost never on campaign; averages of between 40 and 70 seem common. In one typical company at Waterloo - the Grenadiers of the 2/73rd Foot, who had seen hard fighting at Quatre Bras two days before - the record lists two officers and 56 men. (Interestingly, this company of a nominally Scottish battalion first blooded in September 1813 was about 70 per cent English, 20 per cent Irish, and 10 per cent Scottish.)

This cheerful redcoat smokes the short clay "chin-burner" pipe popular throughout the army; the long "church warden" was obviously too fragile, but the shortened type could be stowed with the tobacco pouch, often inside the shako. Tobacco was plentiful in the Peninsula, where all ages and both sexes smoked heavily.

His jaunty forage cap is of the type which officially replaced the earlier "tea-cosy" or "night cap" shapes from 1812 but which was seen in use before that date. It was a knitted, milled cap resembling the Highlanders' "hummel bonnet". The 1812 orders specified a red crown and facing-colour band, but some caps were made vice versa; some, like this reconstruction, had a central company-coloured pompon, and may have been piped.

Left: The 9th Foot demonstrate the redcoat's normal fighting formation: the two-deep line, with the front rank kneeling. The classic confrontation saw the British line waiting unmoved, in disciplined silence, while a cheering column of massed French infantry advanced to close range. At the last moment the redcoats delivered a rapid series of murderous volleys, the line formation allowing every musket in the battalion to be brought to bear simultaneously. Volleys could be delivered in various ways; the battalion was handled, at need, in two, four, eight, 16 or 32 sub-units. Careful timing of orders could produce a virtually continuous rolling fire along the line - although the deafening noise and blinding smoke of battle seldom allowed such perfect control for more than the first few moments. Classically, a few volleys would be followed at once by a howling bayonet charge.

The Foot Guards

(Right, left & right below:)
Recreations of a Light Company, 1st Foot Guards, by a group mainly based in Kent. They wear white overall trousers with the short field gaiters. The "Belgic" shako of 1812-1815 is furnished with the green cords and tuft of Light Infantry; note that this unit wore a buglehorn above, rather than replacing, the cap plate, and this is repeated on the cockade. The 1st Foot Guards wore plain white lace, with "flowerpot" shaped loops set singly, and extra lace edging. Other minor distinctions were their black haversacks, and the buckles on the rear of their accoutrement crossbelts.

The seven battalions of the three Foot Guards regiments of the Napoleonic period were elite units enjoying higher pay. At usually 800 to 1,000 all ranks, the active service battalions were well above the usual Line strength. As Household troops they set high standards of smartness, discipline, and behaviour under fire and on the march.

(Left) A detail from the same action. Note the Foot Guards' distinctions: the sergeant's gold lace, the badge on the pouch flap, and the buckled accoutrement belts. Biting a cartridge in the foreground is a pioneer; these were (and still are) the only men in the battalion traditionally allowed to grow beards. Some Guards units are recorded as wearing white, rather than grey trousers at Waterloo.

(Below) Drummer of the recreated 1st Foot Guards; this group are notable in that they actually issue the private's uniform free of charge to new recruits. The drummer's jacket is elaborately laced in a design peculiar to the regiment, and bears flank company wings - both features still seen today on the ceremonial tunics of Grenadier Guards drummers. The drum was attached to the buff leather crossbelt by a large hook; on the march it could be carried behind the shoulders using the cord slings seen hanging here. The hide apron protected the drummer's leg from the chafing of the swinging drum.Drum and bugle were used extensively for the rapid transmission of the simpler orders on the field of battle; on the march they helped the soldier keep his pace, and in camp they marked the stages of his daily routine.

(Left) The 1st Foot Guards man a redoubt during a re-enactment event at Fort Amherst. This photo perhaps gives some impression of what it must have been like to stand to arms amidst the drifting smoke of battle, with officers and sergeants bellowing the orders to load and fire over the drums' urgent rattle. Drummers were often grown men, but others were certainly boys - in some Napoleonic armies drummers as young as eight were not unknown. No doubt some were soldiers' children born and raised among the camp-followers. Others were orphans, palmed off on recruiters by parish poor-houses eager to escape the responsibility of housing and feeding them.

(Right) The 2nd Bn., 3rd (Scots) Foot Guards fought with distinction at Waterloo, and this figure re-creates the appearance of a Guardsman of the Light Infantry company at Hougoumont on 18 June 1815. The 3rd Foot Guards were identified by pointed-end loops set in threes; and note the bayonet belt plate bearing the star of the Order of the Thistle. The 1812 shako was provided with an oiled fabric cover, with neck flap, for protection in wet weather.

These photos do not, in fact, show a re-enactor, but a model wearing a uniform reconstructed by Gerry Embleton's company Time Machine, which makes life-size historical figures for European museums, to the highest standards of research, materials and finish. This Guardsman is one of a series commissioned by the National Army Museum, Royal Hospital Road, Chelsea, and now on permanent display in the NAM's "Road to Waterloo" exhibition. (Photos: Time Machine Ltd.)

(Above) A snatched impression of the moment of firing during the Fort Amherst re-enactment. After repeated volleys it became hard to control the firing of large bodies of troops in pitched battle. The longer the action, the harder it was for men to synchronise the lengthy reloading process. In close ranks the repeated massed volleys were deafening, even bewildering, and the clouds of choking powdersmoke were as impenetrable as a modern chemical smokescreen. Accounts tell us that in the confusion it was not unusual for men to load more than once without firing, leading to dangerous explosions when they finally pulled the trigger. Others, seeing the enemy nearly upon them, would fire with the ramrod still in the barrel.

Firing flintlocks for any length of time left men with ringing ears, blackened and burned hands and faces, painfully bruised shoulders, and a raging thirst from biting cartridges - black powder rapidly dries up the saliva.

(Right) An officer of the 1st Foot Guards, seen against a drifting bank of powdersmoke, during the annual re-enactment event held at Boulogne in northern France. Although no land actions took place here during the Napoleonic Wars it was the assembly area for the Grande Armée when an invasion of England was contemplated. A number of Napoleonic monuments survive in the area, and each year French groups stage a battle re-enactment and a major parade through the port, which give enthusiasts from all over Europe a chance to come together and share their interests.

(**Left & right**) Probably the best reconstruction of a Light Infantry company sergeant in the country, in the post-1812 uniform of the senior regiment of the British Line: the 1st Foot, Royal Scots. In 1809 this regiment had four battalions totalling more than 4,900 all ranks.

The Royal Scots were re-created by a group based in the Edinburgh region, who spent a great deal of time on the examination of rare surviving items in the collections of the regimental museum and the Scottish United Services Museum; every effort was made to match exact details of materials and cut. (The group now form part of a new European Napoleanic Federation.)

On the 1812 "Belgic" shako the sergeant wears the green cord and tuft of Light troops; on the front are separate Light Infantry buglehorn and regimental number badges; a second buglehorn is fixed through the universal black cockade of Hanover, set over the red cockade of Spain - a regimental distinction marking the valiant service of the 3rd Bn. in the Peninsula, where they fought at Corunna, Bussaco, Fuentes d'Onoro, Badajoz, Salamanca and Vittoria.

The sergeant's jacket is of finer broadcloth, of a brighter scarlet shade, than the almost brick-red of privates' and corporals' jackets; and bears the dark blue facings of all "Royal" regiments. The padded flank company wings, unusually well reproduced here, are in blue rather than red - another regimental distinction, shared only with the Guards. As a sergeant he wears plain white worsted lace, rather than the pattern with an interwoven blue line listed for the rankers of this regiment; the singly-spaced loops were of "flowerpot/bastion" shape from 1812. Note the sergeant's dull crimson worsted sash with a central stripe of facing colour, worn over the accoutrement belts, haversack and canteen. Particular distinctions of Light company sergeants are the rank chevrons worn on both sleeves; and the chained whistle. During the open-order skirmishing away from the main battle line for which these companies were trained, orders were signalled by bugle calls and repeated by officers and sergeants with whistles.

(**Right**) The rear view of this well made and fitted uniform. In Napoleonic times uniforms were delivered to units in bulk once a year, provided by various civilian contractors working more or less closely from the "sealed patterns" provided as working models. The sizing was primitive; and on delivery of the uniforms the (more or less) skilled tailors found in the ranks were excused other duties for weeks of work, unpicking and altering jackets in an attempt to fit the individual soldiers - with varying success. Accounts are full of complaints about the small size, meagre cut and careless workmanship of uniforms supplied by pinch-penny contractors. Inevitably, the soldier's pay was docked to cover the expense of paying the tailors for this extra duty. An ambitious young sergeant like this subject, paid nearly 1s.7d. a day, would certainly have dipped into his own pocket for a superior job.

(Below) A Light company soldier of the Royal Scots in the Line infantry campaign dress of the Waterloo period demonstrates the drill movement for "ram down cartridge". The official drill for loading the Tower musket involved 18 separate steps, from the initial "support arms" to the final "ranks present fire". To achieve three shots a minute in battle many of the finer points would have been disregarded. Ramrods were often stuck in the ground rather than returned to the pipes; and in emergency the musket could be loaded without ramming (providing it was not badly fouled), simply by "jogging" powder and an unwadded "running ball" down the barrel by banging the butt on the ground.

(Above) Sergeants of Grenadier and Battalion companies carried "spontoons" (half-pikes), but since these were obviously unsuitable for open-order skirmishing Light Infantry sergeants carried "firelocks" like their men.

(Below:) Imitating the famous Chez Genty engraving of a soldier of the 5th Foot taken from life during the Allied occupation of Paris, the Royal Scots private has laid down his knapsack. Note the D-section tinned iron messtins in their black oilskin cover, strapped to the blanket roll at the top of the pack. When the commissariat could keep up with the march the soldier received daily up to 1lb. of beef (fresh off the hoof) and 1 1/2 lbs. of bread or hard, weevil-infested "navy" biscuit; he was responsible for cooking for himself (even in barracks). Up to three days' rations were issued at a time and carried in the haversack. Note also the small picker and brush for cleaning the fouling from his musket, carried handy on a chain from his buttonhole.

(Above) Profile of the full marching equipment worn by the Royal Scots private. The haversack was not proofed in any way; in wet weather, or after three days' march in the Spanish summer, raw meat and ration bread would be churned into a stinking mass.

(Above) The heavy, three-pint "Italian" canteen supplied by the Board of Ordnance (hence the painted or branded "BO"and broad arrow). Basically a flat oaken keg, painted blue and often marked with the user's unit and an issue number, it leaked chronically. Soldiers tried to proof them by swirling melted beeswax round the inside; this is reported by re-enactors to give the water a pleasant honey taste. Soldiers were also entitled to a daily issue of a quart of beer, a pint of wine, or a third of a pint of rum; Waterloo memoirs mention issue gin.

(Left) The marching kit worn by a heavily loaded re-enactor of the 68th Durham Light Infantry Display Team, one of the oldest and largest British Napoleonic groups. Note that his greatcoat is worn as a pad between the spine and the infamous Trotter knapsack. "Light" Infantry were so designated only because they were trained to fight - when required - in open order, in a skirmishing screen often pushed out ahead of the main battle line. This screen of Light Infantry and Riflemen, to which Wellington attached great importance, thinned and disrupted advancing enemy formations before they got in range of the main defensive line, and held enemy skirmishers at a distance to prevent them doing likewise. But the Light units were also trained to fight in the line of battle, and carried the same equipment as other infantry apart from a slightly improved model of the Brown Bess.

(Left) Re-enactors representing men of the 2nd Foot (Queen's Royal Regiment) stand sentry outside Fort Amherst in home service dress. The "stovepipe" shako, with its large brass plate, replaced the old tricorne hat in 1800. It was made at first of layers of linen coated with black lacquer, resembling leather. This unsatisfactory cap was itself replaced from 1806 with a felt version with a leather peak. Part of the lining was sometimes brought outside to make a rain flap, and chin tapes could be added.

The 2nd Foot - the old "Tangier Regiment" of the 1660s - fought in the Peninsula at Vimiero, Corunna, Fuentes d'Onoro and Salamanca.

(Below) Off-duty soldier of the Royal Scots wearing the forage cap, and the "sleeved waistcoat" or fatigue jacket which each man was issued for barracks and camp wear. Period engravings show troops on the drill square wearing these jackets with shakos and accoutrements. Made of kersey and serge, sometimes even pipe-clayed white, this jacket had collar, cuffs and sometimes shoulder straps of regimental facing colour. White fatigue overalls made of light canvas ("Russia duck") were also issued as part of the soldier's "necessaries".

This term covered (apart from garments already mentioned) many items for which the soldier had to pay, including two shirts, three pairs stockings or ankle socks (for home or foreign service), a pair of straight-lasted shoes, a pair of breeches slings (braces), two brushes, comb, razor, sponge, soap, shaving brush, towels, mittens, musket tools, cleaning materials, etc. - the list could be greatly extended by unit orders.

The infantry soldier's burden on campaign could reach 75lbs., and was usually at least 60lbs. For men who seem to have been small by today's standards; who were unreliably fed; who marched great distances over appalling dirt roads in the extremes of the Spanish climate; and who, before the general issue of tents in 1813, as often as not slept in the open in all weathers under a single blanket and greatcoat - to these men such loads could be literally fatal. Rifleman Harris, whose memoirs are not the work of a weakling or grumbler, said that "Many a man died, I am convinced, who would have borne up well to the end...but for the infernal load we carried on our backs."

The distribution of the weight was the main problem. Though the canteen, haversack and bayonet more or less balanced the cartridge pouch and slung musket, crossbelts bear down on the chest and shoulders, unlike modern waist-and-shoulder harness which distributes some weight to the hips. Worst of all was the pressure of the knapsack's horizontal chest strap on the ribcage, where it constricted the lungs and caused severe chest pains.

The combination of few (and primitive) roads, and the difficulty of securing enough local wagons and teams to keep the commissariat up with the marching army, meant that the men inevitably had to carry most immediate necessities on their backs. Wellington was more conscious of the problem than most, but there was really no practical solution in the context of those times.

A Fusilier of the 7th Foot recorded the weight carried on the march to Vittoria in 1813, by which date commissariat reforms had made wagon space for camping gear more available: musket and bayonet, 14lbs.; pair crossbelts, 1lb.; pouch with 60 rounds, 6lbs.; full canteen, 4lbs.; three days' rations in haversack, 5lbs.; mess-tin, 1lb.; knapsack, 3lbs.; contents - fatigue jacket $1/2$ lb.; two shirts, $2 1/2$lbs.; pair trousers, 2lbs.; 2 pairs shoes, 3lbs.; two pairs stockings, 1lb; pair gaiters, $1/4$lb.; tent pegs, $1/2$lb.; cleaning and writing kit, $4 1/4$lbs.; greatcoat, 4lbs. Assuming say 3lbs. for the blanket, this totals 55lbs. - on the light side. Often the men also had to share out the various camp "kettles" and tools.

(Above) Men from the 68th pose in the manner of a Charles Hamilton Smith print by a cannon in Berwick barracks, Northumberland. This English Heritage site dates from the 1740s; before the 1790s such purpose-built garrisons were generally found only in threatened regions.

(Left) The 68th on parade. Among the oldest redcoat re-enactment groups, and the largest, the Durhams are not part of the Napoleonic Association but often attend shared events such as those organised at historic sites by English Heritage.

In the foreground is a "chosen man" - the period term for what later became the lance-corporal, but in those days an unpaid appointment made purely within the battalion. Like a corporal's, his chevrons are made from regimental pattern lace, in this case with the 68th's red and green stripes. Such worsted lace in a number of patterns is still manufactured by the Wydean Weaving Co. of Hawarth, West Yorkshire, although it is a special-order item given the limited demand.

(Right) In 1984 Canadian enthusiasts re-created the locally-raised Canadian Fencible Regiment, which fought with distinction against United States forces in the war of 1812-1814 at the battles of Chateauguay, Crysler's Farm, Lacolle Mills and Lake Champlain. There are plentiful surviving records, and the uniforms - exactly like those of Wellington's infantry in the Peninsula apart from details such as button design - are very convincingly reproduced.

A longtime feature of historical re-enactment in North America which is beginning to catch on in Britain is the affiliation of private "living history" groups to museums and other historical sites, to add a new dimension to their appeal to the public.

Here a Light company (left) and a Battalion company private of the re-created Fencibles pose in a period house. They wear the uniform of 1812, with white overall trousers as issued for summer use in several hot-weather overseas stations. (Photo: Janice Lang)

(Left) A pioneer of the 68th. Each battalion had a corporal and ten pioneers, strong men who provided light engineering skills: felling trees, clearing paths, constructing and demolishing barricades, bridges, etc.; and who also slaughtered and butchered the ration beef which was driven on the hoof with the marching columns. Apart from normal musket equipment the pioneers carried billhooks, and each section carried between them three saws, five felling axes, three pickaxes, three mattocks, and eight spades; and in the field they wore leather aprons (see photo right).

(Right) The re-created 68th Foot are known for the scope and care of their historical research; the high standard of their uniforms and equipment; their "living history" encampments; the good order and soldierly discipline with which they conduct themselves; and the accuracy of their well-rehearsed drill and skirmishing displays. They count a number of ex-soldiers among their ranks, which always makes a difference. Here they are inspected by their ensign prior to a skirmish held at the English Heritage site at Scarborough Castle; he wears his fine scarlet melton jacket with the laced, green-faced side of the lapels partly buttoned across, but folded back at the top - a popular style of the Napoleonic period.

(**Below**) Each man was supposed to have two pairs of "strong shoes, shod with nails or plates at the toes and heels, round at toe, and made to come up high round the ankle"; one pair was issued annually and a second bought as part of his "necessaries". On campaign shoes were issued at need when they were (infrequently) available. Ex-cobblers in the ranks carried tools to repair their comrades' shoes. Shoes were made straight-lasted, i.e.there was no difference between left and right.

(**Right**) The Durhams drawn up in the classic two-rank formation, ready to give fire. The 68th was one of the units sent in 1809 on the disastrous Walcheren expedition, which was ravaged by fever: in this battalion 103 men died of it and 599 were shipped home sick, leaving just 76 men "present, fit". Restored to strength (and now more than 40 per cent Irish), they went out to the Peninsula in time for the battles of 1813-14.

(**Above & right**) Impressions of a light infantryman of the 68th on campaign. Note that the short clay pipe was often smoked upside down, to keep the tobacco dry even if the soldier was otherwise soaked to the skin - thus the nickname "chin-burner". The condition of most re-enactors' uniforms does not give anything like a true picture of the state of troops of the period after months of campaigning and hard-lying. Exposed in all weathers, with few opportunities to wash and dry clothing which inevitably suffered from wear and tear and attracted lice, the soldiers sometimes presented such a filthy, patched and ragged appearance that it was hard to tell even their nationality at any distance. They were issued a new jacket once a year at Christmas, and the felt part of the shako; trousers were "necessaries", to be inspected periodically and replaced at the soldier's expense. On campaign they often had to be replaced locally using non-regulation material; Peninsular memoirs speak of brown Spanish cloth, captured blue French trousers, etc. The shoes supplied by contractors were often of poor quality, and in a marching army they always wore out quickly; there are harrowing descriptions of men struggling to keep up with the column, their ruined shoes tied together with bloody rags.

Officers sometimes bought goats at the start of a campaign season, and took them along to provide milk for their tea. This one has no doubt strayed, and is being shown the way home by the nice kind soldier. Ration issue was far from reliable, and was anyway monotonous. Apart from beef and bread (or biscuit, or simply flour) the troops were issued peas, beans, rice, etc. as available. Any further variety was normally a matter for their ingenuity; however, since Wellington relied upon local civilians' goodwill during the Peninsular War he enforced strict regulations against looting from the peasants, in striking contrast to French behaviour. Nevertheless, soldiers let down by the rudimentary supply system often risked the lash or the noose to fill their camp-kettles.

In June 1990 some 2,300 enthusiasts of 26 different nationalities came together at Waterloo to commemorate the 175th anniversary of the climactic battle of the Napoleonic Wars before a huge crowd. Opinions vary on the value of the event as serious historical re-enactment - it was certainly not to be compared in authenticity or organisation with, say, the huge American Civil War battle re-enactments of recent years. But it had its moments; and many who took part in the British ranks recall with pleasure their only opportunity to co-operate with enough other groups to form the classic defensive "square" in something approaching a convincing size.

The "British" square was in fact used by the infantry of many Napoleonic armies as a defence against cavalry charges. The British battalion square was actually a rectangle, with three companies in the front and back faces and two in each side face. Each face of the square was formed of four ranks: the first two kneeling, the second two standing. A battalion with a strength of say 600 men would confront the enemy with 180 men in the front face in four ranks each of 45, about 90 feet long.

Enemy cavalry charging even in fairly tight ranks thus faced at least eight muskets per rider. Horses will not charge straight into any obstacle, let alone a hedge of long bayonets. By controlled firing, the infantry could cut down enough horses and riders to break up the charge well outside the effective range of the cavalry's weapons; once enough of the first rank of the charge had been tumbled over the other horses would always divide and pass by the sides of the square. Squares were ideally drawn up in a checker-board pattern for mutual support.

A square of determined infantry with plenty of ammunition was thus more or less invulnerable against cavalry - unless there was enemy artillery in close support. The square made a perfect target for cannon fire; and the skilful use of cavalry and guns in alternation could do hideous damage to a defensive line of infantry squares. At Waterloo in 1815 some British squares were relentlessly ground away by cannon fire; the survivors drew ever inward to maintain their tight formation, ending up as mere clumps of desperate redcoats, back to back amid a carpet of their dead. But the line never broke...

In the 1990 re-enactment the line was formed by members of the 68th Light Infantry, the 1st Foot Guards, 7th Fusiliers, 9th and 45th Foot, 42nd Highlanders, and about 120 North American redcoats from the 37th, 41st and 49th Foot, the Incorporated Militia and the Fencibles. Re-enactors who stood in square that day recall that after a few volleys had filled the air with dirty powder-smoke, hiding the crowd and the Lion Mound from view, then the sound of drumming hooves growing nearer released satisfactory amounts of adrenalin.

(Left) The 68th Light Infantry parade before the Waterloo re-enactment. Note, immediately left of the King's Colour, a colour-sergeant wearing the sleeve badge introduced for this new rank in 1813.

(Below left & below) At the 1990 re-enactment, as in 1815, weak units came together to form composite squares - thus the three pairs of regimental Colours in the centre of this square, photographed with muskets braced to receive cavalry, and firing a volley. (Photos: Brian L.Davis)

(**Left**) The 68th form a corner, supposedly the most vulnerable place, as the defenders' firepower was divided. In fact nobody has discovered exactly how the ranks were drawn up where companies came together at the corners of squares.

(**Right**) Out of the swirling smoke of battle loom French lancers, making use of their long reach to stab down into the ranks of defenders.

(**Left**) Apart from taking their place in the main line of battle, the regiments of Light Infantry - the 43rd Monmouthshire, 52nd Oxfordshire, 53rd Shropshire, 68th Durham, 71st and 74th Highland, and 83rd Buckinghamshire - provided the army with its protective screen of skirmishers. Sir John Moore presided over a programme of Light Infantry training at Shorncliffe Camp, Kent, early in the century. He encouraged initiative and self-reliance rather than demanding unthinking obedience, appealing to the soldier's pride in his skills and his regiment's crack reputation rather than to fear of the lash. The system paid dividends in the Peninsula, where the Light Infantry proved themselves intelligent, enduring, fast-moving battalions; confident in their superior fieldcraft and marksmanship, they often operated independently of the main army.

Here an officer of the re-created 68th points out a target to his skirmishers. The group practise drill according to the original Light Infantry manuals.

(**Right**) The lofty and the low are one to the brief touch of sharpened steel. As evening falls - at Waterloo, perhaps? - this powder-blackened veteran of the 1st Foot checks his ultimate argument: his 17in. triangular-section socket bayonet. It was not only for stoic defence that Wellington's infantry were famous; in many battles and sieges they showed aggressive bravery in the reckless frontal charge, driving the enemy from the field or the breach at point of bayonet.

The Highlanders

In Scotland at the time of the Napoleonic Wars "going for a soldier" had none of the social stigma attached to military enlistment in England. The Highlands, in particular, were overpopulated, and economic migration was a fact of life. Enlistment was considered an entirely respectable alternative to emigration. The bounties paid to recruits were high, allowing the departing soldier to leave a useful sum for his dependants.

The reason for the generous bounties lay not in any difficulty in finding willing recruits; but rather in the fact that many Scots and English regiments competed for this excellent material, and canny would-be soldiers hung back to compare the various bounties offered by different recruiting parties.

Highland regiments were normally far more homogenous than English ones; while they were not true clan regiments, large numbers of men from the same region would generally be found in the same regiment. A fair number of their officers were often familiar faces, the sons of respected families which had provided local leaders for generations; this led to a high and valuable degree of bonding between officers and their men.

Uneven recruiting and the fortunes of war naturally made it necessary sometimes to fill the ranks from farther afield; but even then Lowland Scots were usually drafted in. It was noticeable that few Irishmen were normally to be found in kilted units, while they often made up 30 per cent or more of nominally English regiments.

The special character of the Highland regiments extended to their behaviour. Although hardy on campaign, spirited in battle, and particularly respected for their ferocity in the assault, they were generally noted for relatively quiet, godly and disciplined behaviour in camp. They were recruited from among independent-minded mountain folk, and obviously were not saints; but links with home communities remained strong; and it was said that the threat of having a notice about his bad behaviour pinned on his kirk door at home was taken more seriously by many a Highlander than fear of the cat o'-nine-tails.

(**Above**) Highlanders of the re-created 42nd (Royal Highland) Regiment stand sentry outside Regents House in Blackheath, London. This English Heritage site is the setting for one of the very impressive period costume balls held towards the end of the summer re-enactment season.

By the 1790s the Highlanders' hose - white stockings with a broad pink/red check, held up by red garters - were normally knitted. They were worn with the usual half-gaiters and shoes.

(**Right**) A "chosen man" and a private of the 42nd in typical marching order; in the background is one of the small "camp colours" used for alignment of bodies of troops and tent lines, usually of the regimental facing colour and bearing some abbreviation of the title.

The most noticeable distinction of the Highland regiments (of which there were up to 15 during the Napoleonic Wars) was of course their uniform. The red jacket, though cut slightly shorter for comfortable wear with the kilt, was basically the same as for other Line units. The kilt was a single length of tartan material, with a central box-pleated section worn to the rear, the two flat "wings" being folded one over the other, the left hand one uppermost, to form a double apron at the front. Accounts show that 3 1/2 yards of 27in. wide material were allowed for a soldier's kilt, 4 yards for a sergeant's - half as much as for modern kilts with their deeper knife-pleats. The 42nd wore the dark blue, green and black sett ("Government" tartan) from which some say they acquired their traditional title, the Black Watch.

(Left) A Black Watch sergeant. Throughout the Line regiments sergeants of Battalion and Grenadier companies carried the spontoon or half-pike; and a sword on the left hip in place of the bayonet - in Highland regiments a basket-hilted Scottish broadsword, in other units a slightly curved sword with a simple brass hilt. The half-pike was more a mark of rank, and an aid in pushing men into alignment, than a weapon, though it came into its own in hand-to-hand fighting.

The "Kilmarnock" bonnet was a pork-pie shaped cap of heavy dark blue wool, knitted and felted; most regiments had a 3in. white band with a red and green checker, and a tufted woollen ball or "tourie" on the crown, in red, white and green for Battalion, Grenadier and Light companies. In some regiments a leather peak was tied on for campaign use. The cockade worn on the left was usually black, though in the 42nd the Grenadiers and Light Infantry wore red and green respectively. The 42nd wore a tall red tuft from the cockade. The bonnet was normally worn unmounted, in so-called "hummel" (humble) style; but for full dress and sometimes on campaign they were seen "mounted" with tall black ostrich feathers. These expensive items easily got lost or damaged, so were often left in stores for safekeeping.

The Highland sergeant's sash was worn over the left shoulder rather than round the waist; and this NCO also wears the tartan plaid brooched to his shoulder - an adornment normally worn by officers, sergeant majors, recruiting sergeants, etc.

(Right) In a haze of powdersmoke, the re-created Black Watch prepare to fire a volley. The oldest and most famous of the Highland regiments, the 42nd fought with distinction in the Peninsula, one or other of its two battalions being present at Corunna, Bussaco, Fuentes d'Onoro, Salamanca, Burgos, and in the invasion of southern France. Reduced to a single battalion, the 42nd fought at Waterloo.

Officers and Gentlemen

The Line battalion was commanded by a lieutenant-colonel, seconded by two majors. Each of the ten companies was led by a captain and two subaltern officers - either lieutenants or ensigns.

In Napoleonic times British officers bought their commissions, and their subsequent promotions, in regiments where there was a vacancy. This system, ludicrous to modern eyes, led to some rich young men holding senior ranks for which they were unfitted, and some battle-proven veterans remaining lieutenants into late middle age. The system had its checks and balances, however; and while some officers were brutal or incompetent, records show that as many were humane, and sometimes outstanding soldiers. The social code of the times at least ensured that no officer who did not show exemplary physical courage had any future with the army.

There was no "regulation" officer's uniform in the modern sense, and regimental tradition or the colonel's whim governed many of the details. The basic uniform before 1812 was a long-tailed scarlet coat faced in regimental colour at collar, lapels and cuffs, laced in either gold or silver according to unit. The lapels could be worn buttoned across showing only the scarlet side; buttoned back on each side of the chest, and closed up the centre with hooks and eyes; or buttoned across apart from exposed triangles of facing at the top. In the Line, pairs of gold or silver bullion wire epaulettes were worn by ranks from major up, single epaulettes by captains and subalterns (Guards, Fusiliers, Light and Highland regiments had their own varied systems).

Other distinctions of officer's uniform were the crescent-shaped gilt gorget worn at the throat on ribbons, and the crimson silk net sash worn at the waist.

Line officers wore a straight sword frogged to a crossbelt with a regimental plate; flank company officers wore sabres; and in practice officers on campaign carried a variety of weapons at personal choice. Breeches, overalls, boots, overcoats etc. were equally a matter for the individual.

Before 1812 the standard Line headgear was a black felt bicorne hat worn "fore and aft"; from that year officers wore the "Belgic" shako, with gilded plate, bullion cords, and a cut feather plume.

(**Left**) A junior officer of the re-created Canadian Fencibles wears the standard uniform of most Line officers from 1812. In that year a short red jacket, similar to that already worn by Light Infantry officers, replaced the long-tailed coat, and the bicorne was replaced by this "Belgic" shako. Note his epaulette, gorget and sash, and the 1796 pattern sword. Bullion lace was usually worn in the same shape and spacing of "loops" as the men's worsted lace, though there were regimental variations. (Photo: Janice Lang)

(**Right**) Each battalion had two Colours of painted silk: the King's Colour, a Union flag, and the Regimental, of facing colour with the Union in the upper hoist canton, both with decorative wreaths and charges showing the regimental name and/or number and sometimes "ancient badges". The Colours were the symbol of the battalion's identity and pride, and the rallying-point in battle. The honourable but dangerous post of colour-bearer fell to ensigns; these two junior officers, often only teenagers, were protected in battle by a guard of at least five sergeants armed with half-pikes. In this photo Canadian Fencibles re-create a famous period plate by Hamilton Smith. In a hot action several ensigns and sergeants in turn might have to replace casualties as they fell. There are many recorded epics of courage in defence of the Colours. (Photo: Janice Lang)

In July 1813, at Wellington's behest, a new rank of colour sergeant was instituted. The senior NCO in each company was marked by a new right sleeve badge: a single chevron below an embroidered crown, Colour and crossed swords.

(**Below & right**) Details of the 68th officer's full dress uniform. The quality of this superb reconstruction underlines the expense officers faced; in Napoleonic times gold and silver lace meant real bullion. At a time when a Line lieutenant's annual pay was about £105, fitting himself out with several sets of "regimentals" to the quality required by his colonel could easily cost a young officer a year's pay. Letters of the day mention a wealthy subaltern buying £300-worth of clothing on joining his regiment; and one fabulously rich captain of the 43rd was reputed to spend £1,000 a year on his wardrobe.

The "stovepipe" shako, in general infantry use by rankers before 1812, was also worn by Light Infantry officers in place of the bicorne. When the "Belgic" shako was introduced in that year for Line officers and men alike, Light Infantry regiments like the 68th retained the old style for all ranks.

The jacket is copied exactly from a surviving original in the Durham Light Infantry Museum. Officers of Light Infantry regiments and companies wore these short jackets instead of the usual long-tailed coat; from 1812 all other infantry officers also adopted the short style.

Note the gorget engraved with the King's cypher, attached to the collar buttons by ribbons of facing colour; this symbol of officer's rank, worn throughout Europe in Napoleonic days, was the last vestige of knightly armour. The 68th officer's swordbelt is adorned with the Light Infantry chained whistle - functional as well as decorative - in addition to a conventional silver regimental plate. Another peculiarity of Light Infantry, seen left, was the special officers' sash with hanging tasselled cords.

The jacket lapels are buttoned back for this order of dress, and fastened invisibly with hooks and eyes. Most regiments were "laced", in gold or silver, though some were not, and exact details varied from regiment to regiment.

(**Above**) An officer of the 68th, wearing superbly reconstructed full dress uniform, rides out with his spaniels; note his white breeches and Hessian boots, and saddle cloth in regimental facing colour laced with silver, with the Light Infantry buglehorn worked in the corner. Infantry officers normally rode when not actually in battle.

Most infantry officers were not members of the aristocracy but of the landed gentry or the then-small professional class; their personal wealth varied widely in an age when an officer needed a private income. Many aspects of his service life were left to his personal means and preference; apart from strictly military duties his army rank was irrelevant - gentlemen did not interfere in one another's personal arrangements.

Even on active service those officers who could afford it lived in some style. They kept strings of horses, and servants; elaborate camping equipment and private supplies of every kind allowed them to pursue a social life, with much entertaining. In their leisure time they shot, coursed or hunted, and several packs of hounds were shipped out to the Peninsula. Some married officers' wives even accompanied them on campaign, with attendant maids and domestic impedimenta.

For impoverished younger officers from more modest middle class families the expense of outfitting themselves was a constant worry - and even more so for the very few ex-ranker officers, who had to struggle to manage on their pay alone. For the men in the ranks a commission by purchase (£400 for an ensigncy) was impossible; but some exemplary long-service senior NCOs were commissioned as quarter-masters or riding masters, and there were cases of rankers being commissioned in the field for acts of outstanding courage in the face of the enemy. (This sequence of photos courtesy Keith Bartlett)

(Left) In place of epaulettes, officers of Light Infantry (and of Grenadier companies and Fusilier regiments) wore "wings", always in pairs; from 1809 officers in these units from the rank of major upward were ordered to wear wings superimposed over pairs of epaulettes. Details of construction varied from regiment to regiment: some wings were partly faced with lace, some with metal scales, others had lengths of chain attached. This careful reconstruction of the 68th style has the only regulation feature - the buglehorn badge. Rank badges on epaulettes were introduced in 1812 for majors and upward.

Some 200 silver bullion "drops" had to be specially made for this meticulous reconstruction, by Hands of London.

(Right) The pockets of Light Infantry jackets were set on "vertically" rather than crossways. The turnbacks of officers' coats and jackets, showing the white lining and edged with regimental lace, often bore decorative badges worked in bullion. For Light companies and regiments these were normally buglehorns; Grenadiers wore a flaming grenade device.

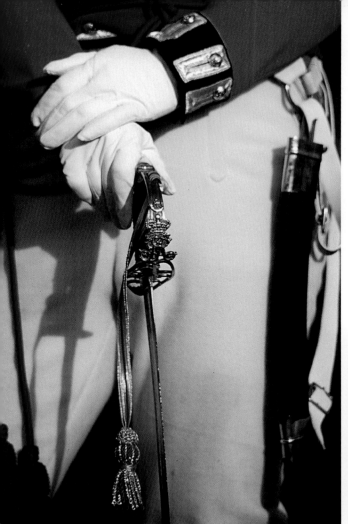

(**Left**) Flank company and Light Infantry officers wore cavalry-style sabres instead of the straight 1796 infantry sword. A regulated pattern was introduced from 1803, with a crowned royal cypher on the guard surmounted by a grenade or - as on this original example - a buglehorn badge. In practice, officers used whatever weapons suited them. The full dress fist strap ("swordknot") was of mixed gold and red for all officers' swords. The sabre was carried suspended from the belt by slings, cavalry fashion, rather than frogged as in Battalion companies. Note the tasselled cords of the Light Infantry sash.

(**Right**) Officers often equipped themselves with less expensive uniforms for battle. This plain, unlaced 68th jacket is worn with typical riding overalls reinforced with leather, and ankle boots. A haversack and small canteen would often be worn; the saddle is padded with a sheepskin, and a bag of oats and a rolled cloak are attached.

Like his uniforms, all campaign equipment fell to an officer's private expense. In the Peninsula scarcity forced up prices for the most necessary articles - a horse could cost £30, a mule for baggage £15-20. The record of one 95th Rifles officer's complete wardrobe (except his regimentals), baggage, tentage, horse and mule suggests a total price of around £100 - a year's pay for a junior officer. Horses and kit often needed replacement due to the hardships of campaign and the fortunes of war.

Greatcoats

During the winter months re-enactors usually content themselves with socialising, study meetings, and the making or repair of uniforms and kit for the coming season. In Napoleonic days, too, most armies preferred to sit out the worst weather in winter quarters - towns, or well-built camps; extremes of weather and the state of unsurfaced roads made major campaigns impractical. Nevertheless, the troops often had to endure rain, icy winds and snow, as during Moore's terrible winter retreat to Corunna in 1808-09; and their only protection was the greatcoat or "watchcloak". (This also comes in handy occasionally for today's re-enactors, such as those who recently ventured to Leipzig, East Germany, in October weather.)

The other ranks' greatcoat was made of dark grey woollen cloth, lined with serge, and cut loosely to fit over full uniform; it was issued in four sizes only. It reached below the knee, and had a standing collar at the base of which was attached a deep cape. The accoutrement belts were worn over the coat but beneath the cape; the coat had shoulder straps to hold them in place. Soldiers often lifted the cape up around the neck and ears in bad weather; and the deep cuffs could also be folded down over the hands.

As the coat was an issue item provided at government expense, the regulations as to when it could be worn were stern, and it was only supposed to be replaced every third year. In practice, since the men very often slept in it in the open air, it wore out far more quickly.

(**Right**) In obviously extreme climates such as Canada the coat was issued every two years. Some troops also received special local issue items, such as the snowshoes worn slung by this patient sentry of the Canadian Fencibles. (Photo: Janice Lang)

(**Above & right**) Re-enactors of the Royal Scots and the Durhams wear the greatcoat with field equipment. NCOs' chevrons could be added to the sleeves.

Although a few regiments had them earlier, before the 1813 season tents were not general issue, and the soldier on campaign slept under whatever shelter he could find or devise. A force of 10,000 to 20,000 men could not all hope to sleep under roofs even when halted in a town or an area of villages; the units often outmarched their baggage trains; and only the most senior officers and their staffs could count on being billeted under cover.

Wooded country offered both shelter and fuel; but much of Spain is not heavily wooded. When benighted in the open soldiers and junior officers became adept at making themselves bivouacs with blankets, muskets, rope, branches, bracken, or anything else useful that they could lay hands on. If the worst came to the worst they simply lay on the ground rolled up in their coats and blankets, with their head or feet thrust into their knapsacks, and shivered the night away as best they could with the aid of alcohol and tobacco. Severe cold and rain cost the army as many sick and dead as the hazards of battle.

(Left) Sergeants added collars and cuffs in facing colour to their greatcoats, and - though hidden here - their chevrons of rank on backgrounds of facing colour. Here a private and a sergeant of the Canadian Fencibles mimic the subject of a period print by Hamilton Smith. (Photo: Janice Lang)

(Right & below) The Canadian Fencibles brave snow and temperatures of -25 Centigrade to re-enact the attack on United States troops at Ogdensburg, New York in February 1813. Records show that the original Fencibles did not receive grey wool campaign trousers until the following year; the re-enactors show their mettle by staying faithful to history even in these conditions. (Photos: Janice Lang)

The Black Brunswickers

Wellington's army in the Peninsula included, apart from British and Portuguese troops, a number of German exile units recruited among nationals of states overrun by Napoleon. The largest contingent was provided by Hanover: the famous King's German Legion, with several excellent battalions of infantry and regiments of cavalry. Uniformed from British stocks, these units served on to make an important contribution at Waterloo.

A smaller corps came from Brunswick; an infantry regiment with a sharpshooter element, and a small hussar regiment, served in the Peninsula from 1810 to 1814. The infantry, the Brunswick-Oels Jaegers (known to the British soldiers as "the Brunswick Owls") fought with several divisions and in a number of engagements. Although the original core were good troops, difficulties in recruiting later gave the unit a fairly motley character.

By 1815 the liberated Duchy had rebuilt its army, and the Duke himself led seven infantry battalions, with cavalry and artillery elements, in the Waterloo campaign. At Quatre Bras the Duke, like his father

before him, fell in battle against the French.

A re-enactment group recruited partly from Germans and partly from US servicemen in Germany re-creates the dramatic appearance of the 1815 Black Brunswickers - specifically the Duke's Leib-Bataillon (Lifeguard Battalion), which was formed around a cadre of Peninsula veterans. **Above,** a company officer leads skirmishers; they wear black uniforms, braided in black, with the light blue facings of the Leib-Bataillon. Their black shakos have tall falling horsehair plumes; and note the sinister white metal death's-head plate, worn by this battalion and the hussars.

(**Right**) A recent addition to the re-created Brunswick Field Corps is a troop of the Hussar Regiment, here represented by a splendidly uniformed trumpeter.

The 95th (Rifle) Regiment

From experience in the French-Indian War in America in the 1750s the British Army had learned the lessons of wilderness fighting. During that conflict, and the War of American Independence 20 years later, companies of light infantry - trained for fieldcraft, mobility and marksmanship, and fitted out with simplified, practical uniforms and equipment - had operated successfully.

Although some regiments maintained integral light companies thereafter, it was not until the Duke of York became Commander-in-Chief of the British Army in 1795 that - among his many other reforms - serious steps were taken to form a true light infantry arm, to counter the very successful use of Chasseurs and Tirailleurs by the French.

It was not until 1800 that the "Experimental Corps of Riflemen" was formed, and its commander Col.Coote Manningham produced the first training manual for the new Light Infantry and Rifle regiments. In 1803 Sir John Moore undertook a training programme at Shorncliffe, Kent, for the 95th (Rifle) Regiment (the former Experimental Corps) and the 52nd and 43rd Foot, newly renamed Light Infantry. Although much of the training was common to all, only the 95th were armed with rifled weapons, the Light Infantry retaining the smooth-bore "Brown Bess".

The principles of the new style training were, for the times, extremely advanced. The ideal, which was certainly achieved to some extent, was that blind obedience enforced by abuse and physical punishment were to be replaced by careful individual instruction in an atmosphere of mutual respect and trust. The officers and men of the Experimental Corps were trained to operate separately as independent companies, which the situation would often demand given their primary role as fast-moving advanced skirmishers and outpost troops.

(**Above**) At the 1990 commemoration of Waterloo, men of the re-created 95th Rifles form a skirmish line ahead of the main British position. This small but respected re-enactment group within the Napoleonic Association have provided advisers for the TV film series based on Bernard Cornwell's "Sharpe" novels.
(Photo: Brian L.Davis)

(**Right**) A 95th Rifleman takes aim, his elbow braced on his knee and his rifle sling braced round his left wrist.

(Left) Rifleman of the 95th aiming his Baker rifle in another "kneeling supported" position, with the ramrod tucked into the hip as a makeshift rest - a comfortable position which can be held for some time without fatigue. Unlike Line troops, the Rifles were trained and equipped for individual marksmanship in a number of standing, kneeling and prone positions; they were even taught to fire lying on their backs with the muzzle between their feet, braced by a foot hooked in the sling.

Note the green uniform peculiar to the Rifles, providing some degree of camouflage; the short unlaced jacket was faced black, with minimal white piping. The haversack, canteen and knapsack were general issue, but the black leather accoutrements were special to the Rifles. They carried a cartridge pouch on a single crossbelt, with made-up ammunition for rapid fire. When possible, they would load with loose powder and separate patch and ball for greater consistency and accuracy; the waist pouch held loose ball, patches were carried in the Baker's brass-covered "butt box", and powder in the small horn strung over the crossbelt.

(Above) The rifle invented by Ezekiel Baker of Whitechapel and adopted for Rifles units had a 30in. spirally-grooved barrel - nine inches shorter than the shortest model of "Brown Bess", though at 11lbs.2oz. it was just as heavy - and a calibre of .615in. compared with .75inch. It shared many of the practical drawbacks of the flintlock musket, although it was much more accurate.

(Right) Each Rifles company was divided into two equal platoons, and these into two equal halves; within each half-platoon a soldier was picked on merit as a "chosen man", marked in the 95th by a white stripe worn around the upper sleeve. He led the squad if no NCO was present, and was next in line for promotion to corporal. In action Riflemen firing prone were taught to use their shakos as rifle rests.

(**Left**) A 95th Rifles bugler fires from cover. Buglers replaced drummers in Rifles units; the emphasis was on speed and mobility - their regulation pace was 140 to the minute (to the Line's 75). The Rifles were taught never to expose themselves unecessarily to enemy fire, but the powder smoke gives away his position however carefully he keeps under cover; he should now move before reloading, if any French skirmishers are within musket range. His rifled weapon gives him the great advantage of effective accuracy at 300 yards, three times the accurate range of a smooth-bore.

(**Right**) The re-created 95th Rifles search enemy dead in the midst of a skirmish. Note the sergeant's sash - scarlet rather than the Line's crimson, and with a black central stripe; and his chevrons of rank on the right sleeve - all the 95th's NCO ranks used white tape. Riflemen were the only troops to wear cords on the "stovepipe" shako, though such decorations often became lost on campaign.

Looting, and often stripping of the dead is, to modern eyes, one of the more squalid aspects of Napoleonic campaigning; but the soldiers of all armies of the day accepted it as a matter of course. The attitude to plundering even ones own fallen comrades was severely unsentimental: the dead had no further need of their possessions and kit, while food, an extra shirt or a spare pair of shoes might make all the difference for the living. Any fallen enemy officer would quickly loose his watch, purse, and probably the epaulettes and any gold lace easily removed from his uniform.

(**Right**) Skirmishing was always carried out in pairs, so that one man was always ready to fire while the other reloaded. Within each company men paired off with their "rear-" or "front-rank man", and could not be separated without the commanding officer's permission; they served, marched and messed together, in barracks and in the field.

Reloading was taught in standing, kneeling and prone positions, and on the move - though it was difficult when prone. It took longer to reload the Baker rifle than a musket, because the patched ball fitted much more tightly into the grooved barrel; initially the Riflemen were issued a small mallet to tap the ramrod, but this was apparently unpopular and later discarded.

On the left hip is frogged the Baker's 24in. brass-hilted sword bayonet, which attached to the muzzle by a spring clip to give the Rifleman the same reach as a man with a musket. It was apparently unpopular, as the rifle could not be fired with the sword fixed, and it was probably used more as a camping tool than a weapon.

(Above left & right) An officer of the 95th Rifles. All Light Infantry had a reputation for dash and glamour, and the Rifles were a particular novelty; this was reflected in the officers' uniforms, which seem to have displayed a range of individual taste, including light cavalry features. The peakless shako with a folding flap at the front, resembling the old 18th century hussar mirleton cap, is decorated with cord, a cut-feather plume, and a buglehorn badge. The green jacket is lavishly decorated with black cord braiding, and is faced with black velvet. There are three rows of silver buttons, ball-shape down the centre and half-ball each side. Like cavalry, these officers wore a pouch-belt, the pouch flap decorated with the buglehorn (which was taken as a badge by the light troops of most armies in reference to the traditional hunting horn of the German "jaegers").

(Right) On campaign Rifles officers seem often to have covered or replaced their tight green breeches with cavalry-style overalls reinforced with leather. Note the Light Infantry sash; the sabre; and the small folding telescope - a campaign necessity for all officers.

(Above left & right) Another reconstruction of a 95th officer's uniform, worn during the 1990 Waterloo commemoration. This is a copy of the surviving jacket of Capt. Walter Clarke now in the regimental collection of the Royal Green Jackets. Note the black braiding carried right over the shoulders and round the back of the neck - as far as is known this is probably Clarke's personal affectation; but it is typical of the flamboyance of the "Light Bobs". (Photos:Brian L.Davis)

(Right) Reconstructed campaign dress of an officer of the 5th Battalion, 60th Rifles, distinguished from the 95th by his red jacket facings - and note the cavalry overalls and barrel-sash. There is period evidence for the use of the hussars' heavily laced, fur-trimmed pelisse over-jacket slung from one shoulder by some Rifles and Light Infantry officers.

The 60th were originally raised as the Royal American Regiment during the French-Indian War, largely from German and Swiss immigrants who supposedly had forest experience. Enlarged over the years, it was always a foreign mercenary unit intended for overseas service. The 5th Bn., raised largely from German volunteers in 1798, served in Ireland, the West Indies, South America, and Canada. Between 1808 and 1814 it fought in the Peninsula, where it was normally split up into dispersed companies to thicken up the skirmishing line of various divisions with expert riflemen.

It was part of Moore's policy at Shorncliffe that officers were not supposed to exchange between companies, remaining with their men over long periods so that all ranks became accustomed to one another; each company's officer strength was kept the same, and officers were trained to lead dispersed companies on independent operations.

The Cavalry

The British cavalry during the Napoleonic era was composed of two distinct types of troops, Heavy and Light, the former including the three regiments of the Household Cavalry. The heavy regiments were the older form, tracing their origins to the aftermath of the English Civil War. The 17th and early 18th century mounted regiments were designated as either "horse" or "dragoons"; the former were line-of-battle cavalry in the classic sense, the latter mounted infantry who rode to battle and dismounted to fight on foot. As time passed this distinction became blurred, and by the Seven Years' War in the mid-18th century dragoons were for all practical purposes identical to the rest of the mounted arm. By the Napoleonic Wars only their title set them apart.

During the 1740s the Continental concept of light cavalry had reached Britain, and a short-lived Light Dragoon regiment was raised. In 1756 a "light troop" was added to most cavalry regiments; and in 1759 the first permanent regiment was raised - Elliot's, later the 15th Light Dragoons. Their brilliant success at the battle of Emsdorf vindicated the experiment, leading to the formation of further regiments of Light Dragoons, and to clearly defined roles for heavy and light cavalry.

The heavy horse - whose mounts, usually from Ireland and known as "cavalry blacks", were of the type used to this day by the Mounted Squadron of the Household Cavalry - were line-of-battle regiments, used for shock action and the exploitation of breakthroughs. The mission of the light regiments - riding only slightly smaller bays, duns and chestnuts - was the "war of outposts": patrolling and probing, riding flank protection and rearguard on the march, extending the army's vision and reach over the horizon (although they were still capable of taking their place in the main line of battle at need).

A recruit wishing to enlist had a wide choice. The elite of the heavy horse were the Household regiments - the 1st and 2nd Life Guards and the Royal Horse Guards. There were seven numbered regiments of Dragoon Guards, and five of Dragoons (1st to 6th - the 5th had been disbanded). The Light Dragoons were numbered from the 7th upwards, rising to the 29th by the end of the period. Four of these - the 7th, 10th, 15th and 18th - bore the secondary title "Hussars".

The structure of the regiment was much the same whatever the designation. Each was divided into eight to ten troops, each of approximately 80 to 90 men led by a captain and three subalterns; on campaign pairs of troops would form squadrons, but this was a field formation only. A regiment posted overseas would have three or four sabre squadrons, leaving a depot squadron at home. On campaign, however, the actual strength was often far below establishment; and keeping regiments provided with remounts was a constant problem.

1st Life Guards

The introduction of cavalry into the world of Napoleonic re-enactment is new to the United Kingdom. Would-be cavalry re-enactors face serious obstacles: the cost, the logistic problems, the recruiting of competent riders, and the location of suitable venues for mounted displays are only the most obvious. The Napoleonic Association is many years behind the Sealed Knot and English Civil War Society in this respect. However, over the last three years all three main types of period cavalry have made their appearance in embryo, if only with half-a-dozen riders each: the Life Guards representing the heavy horse, the Light Dragoons, and the Hussars. Given the high standards achieved by all three groups, even a small number of well-mounted, well-appointed riders make a fine spectacle; and despite some initial grumbles from the infantrymen about the expense of hiring horses, the cavalry have been accepted as an integral part of re-enactment events.

(Above) Mounted private of the 1st Life Guards Waterloo Troop giving his officer the typical salute of the period.

(Right) Two Life Guards officers resplendent in their finer quality uniforms: bright scarlet coatees, large feather plumes, gold shoulder cords and gold laced girdles.

This re-enactment group have achieved a great deal in a short time, by a considerable research effort and much hard work; these photos speak for themselves. Much work still needs to be done on the reconstruction of saddlery, a major problem for all cavalry impressions; the horse shown above is fitted out with a First World War bridle and bit for lack of correct reconstructions - which will no doubt come with time. The horse is a dark bay; various colours were ridden by most units by 1800, but though the "cavalry black" was retained by the Household and other senior regiments it is simply not available for re-enactment purposes today.

(Below) The trumpeter of the 1st Life Guards Waterloo Troop affords us a closer look at the fine detailing of the Grecian-style helmet; the Life Guards and Royal Horse Guards wore it with this stuffed woollen roach in dark blue and red, the Line heavy cavalry with a flowing black horsehair mane. The reconstructed helmets are the result of months of painstaking work by a model figure sculptor; working from an original helmet in the Life Guards museum, and picking out every detail with a scalpel, he produced a perfect model from which a mold was made for casting.

In January 1813 a brigade comprising two squadrons each of the 1st Life Guards, 2nd Life Guards and Royal Horse Guards joined Wellington's Peninsula field army, and served until the end of the campaign. The Duke praised their steadiness and discipline - and given his jaundiced view of the generally brave, well-mounted but fatally undisciplined British cavalry,

his praise is significant. In too many of the Peninsula battles the carelessly officered cavalry would charge with great spirit; but - like Prince Rupert's cavaliers 150 years before - would get themselves cut up, or dispersed over miles of countryside, through failing to obey the recall trumpets. The Duke judged them worth twice their strength in French cavalry once it came to a confrontation, but could seldom trust them to be where he wanted them when they had once been let off the leash.

In the Waterloo campaign the Household Brigade, under Gen.Lord Edward Somerset, consisted of around 230 each from the 1st and 2nd Life Guards and the Royal Horse Guards, with 530 men of the 1st King's Dragoon Guards. The 1,200 heavy horsemen saw fierce fighting in a number of engagements, mostly with French Cuirassiers and Carabiniers; and by the end of the day could muster only a single composite squadron.

(Above & right) The 1st Life Guards' trumpeter/corporal of horse and two privates display various details of their uniform and equipment. The serviceable short-tailed campaign service coatee, of a brighter scarlet than Line privates' uniform, is based on careful examination of a surviving example now in the National Army Museum, said to have been worn at Waterloo by one Lance-Corporal Gill. Laced gold for all ranks, its "Royal" blue facings are seen as collar patches, shallow cuffs, turnbacks, rear-set shoulder straps, and piping.

Note the width of the men's

whitened buff leather equipment belts; the yellow and red worsted girdles; the striped overalls; the long, straight 1796 heavy cavalry pattern sword in its steel sheath; and the star badge fixed through red backing to the cartridge pouch flap. Heavy cavalry were issued with a carbine and saddle pistols.

These photos of the Waterloo Troop were taken at one of the "living history" events during which the group carry out their stable duties, provide mounted sentries, and demonstrate the cavalryman's daily duties in camp.

(**Below**) A Life Guards officer (right) wearing the large black felted bicorne hat of pre-1812 uniform (and doubtless still worn after that date by officers not actually parading with troops), and the richly laced and embroidered pouch belt, pouch flap, sword belt slings and sabretasche of full dress uniform. He is being saluted by an aide de camp in the 1815 uniform of the 7th (Queen's Own) Light Dragoons (Hussars); this officer wears an individually reconstructed uniform - the 7th Hussars do not yet exist as a re-enactment group.

(**Above**) The surgeon of the 1st Life Guards Waterloo Troop, Malcolm MacDonald; his fascinating lectures on the medical services of the day, illustrated with his collection of period instruments, are a feature of the "living history" aspect of the hobby. Medical officers were supposed to provide themselves with rather plain single-breasted scarlet uniform coats faced with black, and were further identified by black hat plumes and sword belts; in practice a mixture of medical and regimental uniforms seem to have been worn. This peaked forage cap would be typical of officers' wide latitude in the choice of off-duty headgear.

*   *   *

One duty of the regimental surgeon was to be present to witness corporal punishment. Any but the most minor misbehaviour might earn a soldier a flogging with the cat-o'-nine-tails; the colonel of a unit could award sentences of anything up to 500 lashes. Some colonels despised flogging, and avoided it whenever possible; others were tyrants who made their men's lives a burden.

For "flogging at the triangle" the soldier was stripped to the waist and tied to a tripod, made in the infantry by lashing together a number of sergeants' half-pikes. The flogging would be carried out with a scourge made from nine knotted leather thongs (see the reconstruction of these in the photo above right). The cat would be wielded by one or more of the drummers or trumpeters, in relays if many lashes were awarded, while the sergeant-major kept the count.

The surgeon was present to inform the colonel if he judged that the victim's life was in danger. If he did so the man was cut down; his back (on which the flesh might by that stage be so mangled as to expose the bone) was washed with salt water; and he was taken away to recover - until fit enough to be triced up again to suffer the rest of his sentence...

Apart from being terribly scarred for life, the victim of a long flogging might be crippled, or suffer internal injuries. (There are men alive today who suffered a "mere" 12 or 18 lashes with the cat in HM Prisons, where flogging was awarded for attacks on warders until 1968; they recall the shocking impact of the blows, apart from the cutting effect.)

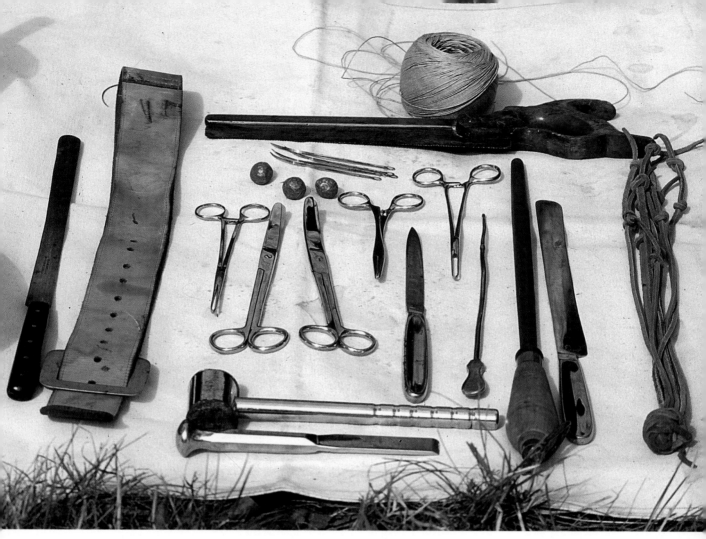

(Above) A selection of period surgeon's instruments - these particular examples were once the property of a surgeon working at a city mortuary: a chisel and saws for bone and flesh, probes for use when searching wounds for musket balls, a leather tourniquet for amputations, a variety of scalpels, knives and forceps, needles, catgut, etc. - and at right, the lash from a cat-o'-nine-tails.

The army medical services of the day were rudimentary. Rear hospitals were often grisly lairs of ignorance and neglect, and breeding-grounds of disease; soldiers dreaded them for finishing off more wounded and sick than they saved. Unlike the French, whose Surgeon-General Baron Larrey instituted purpose-built ambulances among his many humane reforms, the British transported the wounded who survived immediate treatment on long, agonising journeys in unsprung wagons and ox-carts.

Most surgery was carried out at regimental level. Each unit was supposed to have one surgeon (a qualified doctor) and two assistants; there were no trained orderlies, and members of the band were traditionally given the duty of helping the wounded back to an improvised aid post close behind the fighting line. A major battle left the wounded lying where they fell for hours, even days, at the mercy of the weather - and looters.

While many of the grossly overworked surgeons were as conscientious and humane as the impossible conditions allowed, their general standard of knowledge was not high; there were many complaints about their ignorant butchery, and it was not a job to attract any medical man with the skill to found a lucrative practice. Given contemporary ignorance of the principles of infection, the massive wounds inflicted by Napoleonic weapons, the absence of anaesthetics, and the general lack of sanitation, even the best doctors owed most recoveries from battle trauma (and there were many) to luck and the patient's constitution.

Sword cuts healed easiest, as they seldom carried dirt into the wound; there are records of men recovering from up to a dozen gruesome slashes.Cut and punctured wounds were usually simply sewn, dressed, and left to heal as they might. Infection might be treated by live maggots being bound into the wound for up to 48 hours to eat the mortifying flesh.

Penetrating gunshot wounds in the torso usually became infected by foreign objects and dirt carried in, with fatal consequences. The shock and blood loss caused by deep probing for the ball without anaesthetic killed many; surgeons often left deeply sited balls in the body and trusted to luck.

Gunshot wounds to the limbs often caused severe splintering of the bones. Surgeons knew the dangers of gangrene, and usually opted for amputation; some thought it best to wait to let the patient build up his strength, but most felt it best to cut straight away while he was still in shock from his wound. The patient would be given a gulp of issue rum and held down on a bloody makeshift operating table. Some surgeons prided themselves on the speed with which they could take off a limb; but sometimes it could take up to 20 minutes.

There are many horrific accounts by amputees; their stoic endurance is astonishing to modern readers - as is the number who recovered. One aggravating factor was the British practice (presumably for the sake of speed) of cutting straight round the limb without taking time to flay back enough skin to form generous flaps over the stump - as was the French practice; many British amputees suffered further agonies, and fatal post-operative infection, when the later expansion and contraction of the remaining muscles burst the wound.

(**Left & below**) The regiments of Dragoon Guards and Dragoons wore from 1812 a short red coatee fastened with hooks and eyes, with facing colour at collar, shoulder straps, cuffs and on the small turn-backs, and trimmed with broad double lace. The reinforced riding overalls were striped in various ways; the Greys had two blue stripes and a row of buttons. Note the broad worsted waist girdle, and sergeant's gold chevrons worn on the right sleeve only.

Raised in the 17th century as the Scots Dragoons, the regiment were known as the Greys (from their original uniform colour) by 1700; they rode grey horses from an early date, and by the Napoleonic period were unique in the army for this practice. They did not serve in the Peninsula; but their charge at Waterloo became one of the British Army's great legends.

With the 1st Royal Dragoons and the 6th Inniskilling Dragoons they formed Gen.Ponsonby's Union Brigade, providing three squadrons - about 390 men. When the first massed French infantry attack by D'Erlon's four divisions had been checked by the fire of Picton's veteran infantry Wellington's cavalry commander, Lord Uxbridge, ordered the two heavy brigades to charge.They smashed into the enemy corps, driving them back in confusion with great loss; it was during this action that Ewart captured his eagle.

Sadly, the battle-maddened troopers failed to obey the recall, and charged on deep into the French lines to cut down enemy artillerymen among their guns. Cut off by French cavalry including lancers, and with their formation broken up, they had to fight their way back against odds: Gen.Ponsonby was killed, the Greys' Col.Hamilton was never seen again, and in all the regiment lost some 200 dead and wounded.

(**Left**) A reconstruction, by Gerry Embleton's Time Machine Ltd., of the 1815 service dress and marching order of the Royal Scots Greys - officially, the 2nd (Royal North British) Dragoons. The uniform was reconstructed for Time Machine's figure, in the National Army Museum exhibition, of Sgt.Ewart, the Waterloo hero whose capture in hand-to-hand fighting of the eagle standard of the French 45th Line Infantry earned the Greys their later cap badge.The fearsome hatchet-pointed 1796 heavy cavalry sword which Ewart wielded in the battle can be seen today in the regimental museum at Edinburgh Castle.

The re-created "Sgt.Ewart" wears the peaked bearskin cap unique to the 2nd Dragoons, protected from the weather, as it was at Waterloo, by an oilcloth cover. (Photos: Time Machine Ltd.)

(Right) Rear view of the Scots Greys sergeant in marching order. The heavy cavalry wore their long straight sword from a waist belt and two slings, with a plain black sabretasche - a large flat pouch, still used by officers for carrying writing materials, but for rankers largely decorative. A broad whitened belt of "buff" leather was fitted with a pouch on inner attachments for 30 pistol and carbine cartridges (the pouch slightly curved to fit snugly when on the march), and a swivel hook for the carbine itself. The ration haversack and water canteen were of the same type as issued to the infantry, worn higher up under the left arm - but re-enactors can confirm that they still flap and bang alarmingly when trotting.

12th (Prince of Wales's) Light Dragoons

The re-created 12th (Prince of Wales's) Light Dragoons are a unit of the Napoleonic Association who work closely with English Heritage. They take part in the small but very high quality English Heritage events entitled "Wellington's Army", with other particularly authentic groups such as the 68th Durhams and the 95th Rifles. The 12th Light Dragoons have also turned out in the past (with obvious adjustments) in the guise of the Polish lancers of Napoleon's Vistula Legion, providing the redcoats with an "enemy"; steps are now under way to re-create a French Line lancer unit within the Napoleonic Association.

(Right) A "chosen man" in the 1812 uniform of the 12th LD prepares to mount. He wears home service dress, with white breeches and Hessian boots. Before 1812 Light Dragoons were uniformed rather similarly to Hussars, with a richly braided dolman jacket and breeches; their headdress was a handsome leather "Tarleton" helmet with a black bearskin crest. From that date this new uniform appeared, with a felt shako, and a dark blue jacket of the so-called "Spencer" cut inspired by that of the French lancers. Each regiment had a different combination of facing and lace colours: for the 12th, yellow with white. Note the swivel hook, ring and bar attachment for the carbine worn slung from the crossbelt.

The regiments of Light Dragoons made up the bulk of Wellington's cavalry in the Peninsula; this "all purpose" light horse was the most practical type of cavalry for the terrain and the range of operations. At one time or another the 11th, 12th, 13th, 14th, 16th, 18th, 20th and 24rd served in Portugal and Spain. The 12th (Prince of Wales's) went out in time to fight at the great battles of Salamanca and Vittoria in 1812 and 1813; and fought with Vandeleur's Brigade at Waterloo.

Wellington had three major problems with his cavalry: finding enough good forage to keep British-bred horses in condition; finding a steady supply of remounts; and finding competent - rather than merely dashing - commanders. In those years the British Army really had only two first class cavalry generals, Uxbridge and LeMarchant.

(Photo: Martin Pegler)

(Left) Rear view of the 1812 Light Dragoon uniform, showing the very French cut of the "Spencer" jacket. Note the small "waterfall" of worsted fringing in the small of the back, showing beneath the girdle. Another radically un-British feature was the wearing of epaulettes by all ranks - in worsted fringing for privates and NCOs. The cap lines from the shako passed under these, the decorative knots attaching to a button to prevent the loss of the headgear if it came off while riding.

Preparing to mount, this man has passed his slung carbine up and back over his shoulder to keep it out of the way. The 1796 light cavalry sabre and the plain sabretasche each hang by two slings from rings on the sword belt, which is concealed under the jacket. Getting into the saddle with all this kit dangling around the legs is a knack which takes time to learn.

This view shows the very well reconstructed 1812 light cavalry bridle, with fancy rosettes and crossed facepieces in Hungarian style; and the breastplate harness which prevented the 1805 light cavalry saddle from slipping backwards. (Photo: Martin Pegler)

(Left) The "chosen man" in the saddle; a single white lace chevron on regimental yellow backing is worn on his right sleeve only. The sheepskin, edged with vandyked cloth in regimental colour, is for comfort. Behind the saddle the tubular cloth valise containing his personal kit has a regimental cypher applied in worsted lace; below it is a horseshoe case; and his rolled cloak is strapped at the front of the saddle.

He braces the so-called "Paget" carbine issued to Light Dragoons and Hussars (in this case an original weapon). Introduced gradually from 1800, it is 2ft.7ins. long, of .65in. calibre, weighs 5lbs., and has a swivel ramrod permanently attached by a swinging link at the muzzle.

The 1796 pattern Dragoon carbine issued to the heavy cavalry was 3ft.5 1/2ins. long, of full musket calibre (.75in.), and weighed around 8lbs. Originally the heavy cavalry had pistols of .75in. calibre, but they too received the .65in. New Land Pattern from about 1802. (Photo: Martin Pegler)

(Above) Apart from sabre and carbine the cavalry, heavy and light, were also armed with a pair of New Land Pattern flintlock pistols holstered at the front of the saddle, butts forward; they were of the same calibre as the light cavalry carbine, so common ammunition could be carried, and like the carbine had an attached swivel ramrod. This view shows how awkward it must have been to draw a pistol with any speed from beneath the cloak roll. Here the carbine is carried by a strap to the front of the saddle, its muzzle in a small "boot". (Photo: Martin Pegler)

(Above & left) English Heritage naturally demand a very high standard of horsemanship from any mounted re-enactment unit which performs in front of the public, for safety reasons. Handling the weapons and equipment of a Napoleonic trooper close to a crowd demands serious training; and the re-created 12th Light Dragoons are all expert riders - several of them in fact hail from His Britannic Majesty's colonies in the Antipodes. Part of their programme for the public is an impressive skill-at-arms display with the 1796 light cavalry sabre, the New Land Pattern pistol, and - from the 1994 season - the carbine.
(Photos: Mike Groves & Linda North)

(Right) A private of the 12th Light Dragoons in campaign dress prepares to mount; he wears leather-reinforced riding overalls, an oilcloth shako cover, a haversack and a canteen. The linen bag on the saddle contains a supply of oats for the horse. Light cavalry do not seem to have ridden horses very much smaller than the "heavies": records show that the norm for both the 10th Light Dragoons and the Scots Greys was 15 to 15 1/2 hands.
(Photo: Martin Pegler)

(**Left**) A light dragoon on vedette in the cold morning light. Note that the plastron of his jacket is buttoned across, for warmth and to hide the bright facing colour. Behind the stirrup hangs a hay net. At the end of the day's march the cavalryman was allowed either to replenish this from the supply wagons or to go and forage for it himself.

Each horse was supposed to get 14lbs. of hay or straw, and 12lbs. of oats or ten of corn, every day; and keeping them fed in the less fertile regions and seasons was a problem which directly affected the army's ability to manoeuvre and fight. Cavalrymen were constantly ranging the countryside for miles around the column, foraging for fodder with reaping-hooks, nets and mules.

During the Peninsular War huge supply columns were needed to carry fodder and fuel for the army on the march - 10,000 mules and donkeys, in addition to purely regimental transport, was not an unusual figure. At regimental level a cavalry unit had a considerable logistical "tail"; the 400-odd men were allowed one baggage mule for every two men and horses, and would need another 300 commissariat mules to maintain their animals. There was an allocation of one and a half supply wagons for each troop; three more for the surgeon and veterinary, paymaster and adjutant, and regimental stores; saddler's, armourer's, and forge wagons; the column also included the officers' baggage carried by bat horses, and strings of spare mounts.

(**Right**) A good rear view of the 12th Light Dragoon's marching order from the near side.

15th (King's) Light Dragoons (Hussars)

The 15th Light Dragoons were the first British regiment to be formed specifically as light cavalry and to remain permanently on the army list. Five more new light cavalry regiments were raised during the Seven Years' War, at a time when the Eastern European concept of light horse was becoming increasingly influential throughout the Continent. The term "hussar", and the elements of a romantic uniform style which was soon internationally recognised and copied, were derived from the irregular light horse originally recruited to serve on the wild fringes of the Austro-Hungarian Empire. The new British light regiments had from the start a fashionable, dashing image; and by the end of the 18th century some of them had unofficially adopted some elements of the hussar uniform style.

In 1805 the trend was officially recognised by an order instituting full hussar dress for the 7th, 10th and 15th Light Dragoons, soon followed by the 18th - although, ever-conservative, Horse Guards only added the Hussar designation in brackets after the regimental title. Their tactical role remained identical to that of the Light Dragoons: long range patrolling, ambush and raiding, intelligence gathering, and screening the army, as well as fighting in the line of battle.

The author must declare an interest, as a member of the small re-enactment unit which now re-creates the 15th Hussars; but believes that these photos speak for themselves as to the quality of their reconstructed uniforms. Though newcomers to the Napoleonic re-enactment scene (as are all the cavalry impressions), they are confident in their research and the standard of the reproduced items. Virtually all of these have been based on surviving items held in the collection of the regimental museum; without the help of its curator, former Sgt.Maj.Ralph Thompson, the project to re-create the colourful past of the old 15th Hussars would not have been possible.

The members of the group are all experienced horsemen; less experienced riders may carry out foot duties while they learn the skills necessary to take part in high quality skill-at-arms displays such as "running the ring" and the "course of heads".

(Left & right) The fantastic full dress uniform of the first generation British hussar. The towering fur busby was always worn at a dashing tilt, so that the red cloth bag and the yellow cap lines could swing freely with a little swagger. The tight-fitting dolman jacket, tailored to show off the figure to best advantage and heavily braided front and rear, shows the 15th's red facings at collar and cuff. Tight buckskin breeches and Hessian boots were traditionally associated with hussar costume; as was the "barrelled" sash, here in crimson wool and plaited yellow worsted.

The rear view displays the fur-trimmed pelisse over-jacket in all its glory. In the 15th it was trimmed with black sheepskin and lined with red worsted. Worn over the dolman in winter, it was essentially a parade item in summer, worn slung flamboyantly from the left shoulder.

(Above) The hussar as he would have appeared on winter campaign service in 1808-09, when the 15th formed part of Sir John Moore's army on the retreat to Corunna. The busby, measuring a full 12ins. tall and originally worn without the aid of chinscales, was an imposing but fairly unsatisfactory headdress - as members of the re-enactment group have found out while on horseback. After Corunna it was drastically reduced in height and given chinscales to secure it. The pelisse is worn over the dolman for warmth, and leather-reinforced overalls complete the outfit.

The hussar holds an example of the deadly 1796 light cavalry sabre from the regimental museum. This particular sword was carried throughout the Corunna campaign and was used in the cavalry action at Sahagun on 21 December 1808, in which Lord Paget's hussars routed twice their number of French cavalry; it bears the marks of heavy use, and is notched and scarred along its entire length.

(**Right**) A mounted hussar in the campaign dress and kit of the first year of the Peninsular War. The elaborate shabraque was reserved for more formal occasions, and on campaign the saddle was covered with a sheepskin edged with coloured cloth cut in a vandyke style. The curved cartridge pouch fits snugly under the arm.

(**Opposite**) Near-side view of the hussar private. Note that the steel scabbard of the 1796 sabre was painted black for campaign service to protect it from rust. No commercial copies of the sabre are yet produced; luckily original weapons are still fairly widely available at arms fairs across the country. Given the bewildering amount of uniform, equipment and saddlery involved in reconstructing an impression of a Napoleonic cavalryman, and the consequent expense, the prospective recruit is kitted out by the group free of charge on joining the 15th Hussars.

(**Right & opposite**) A striking impression of an officer of the 15th Hussars on campaign, wearing a painstaking copy of an original uniform. The square-section silver cording on the dolman and the crimson and gold barrelled sash were specially commissioned from the Wydean Weaving Company of Hawarth, West Yorkshire. Officers wore more elaborate plumes, bullion cap lines, and overalls with tan rather than black leather inserts; and used black rather than white sheepskin saddle covers. The impression even of this relatively simple field uniform emphasises the fact that the light cavalry attracted the wealthiest families. The price of a cavalry lieutenant's commission was nearly £1,000, that of a captaincy nearly £3,000; and his uniforms could cost huge aditional sums.

Note, again, the reconstruction of the Hungarian-style 1812 light cavalry double bridle, with both a small ringed snaffle and a curb bit.

(Right) Stable dress was much the same for all light cavalry regiments. The "watering" cap had a band in regimental facing colour, which was also displayed on the cuffs and as collar patches on the simple blue stable jacket. This was a straight-waisted, single-breasted item, with about ten small pewter buttons and two waistcoat-type pockets; the cuffs were always pointed in the light cavalry (and cut straight in the heavy regiments). For all orders of dress NCOs in the 15th Hussars wore a crown above their chevrons from 1801 onwards. The troop sergeant's chevrons are in Royal pattern lace - yellow with a blue stripe - on a backing of facing colour.

(Below) The Napoleonic cavalryman enjoyed higher pay than his infantry comrades, and - given his much greater range of kit - received more of it free from deductions and stoppages; but he worked hard for it. The cleaning, grooming, feeding, watering and general care of the horse always came first, in barracks or in the field. Large numbers of horses were inevitably lost on campaign due to their vulnerability to illnesses and disorders, long marches, heavy burdens, bad weather and uncertain supplies of adequate fodder, apart from the hazards of battle; but whenever humanly possible the British Army traditionally took far greater care of their mounts than the French, and this policy paid dividends in battle.

The would-be Napoleonic Wars cavalry re-enactor should not underestimate the number of hours of sheer labour with which he must pay for his brief glory in front of the public. His horse, too, needs constant supervision and care; and dull, laborious hours must be spent cleaning the various items of tack and equipment, soaping the leatherwork, and polishing all the many buckles and fittings. All the groups demand the high standards of dedication appropriate to their historical subjects; the cavalry is not the place for the "beer and bash" type of re-enactor.

(Right) The troop sergeant poses
in the full splendour of the 15th
Hussars' post-1812 summer
campaign dress. The red shako
remained in use by the 15th until
the 1850s, when it was replaced
in its turn a new model of the
busby.

(Above) Early in 1812 the 15th
Hussars replaced their fur busbies
with this striking new headgear:
the leather-topped Light Dragoon
shako of that year's pattern, with
the standard lace top band and
"wheel", but with a scarlet cloth
body. The busby had been
inspired purely by fashion; the
shako - worn here with the pelisse
in winter campaign dress - was a
much more practical headgear,
giving some protection against
sabre cuts, and shade for the eyes.

80

(**Right**) One English Heritage event gave us this opportunity to re-create, with the aid of members of the 68th Durham Light Infantry Display Team and the 95th Rifles, one of Charles Hamilton Smith's famous contemporary print series "Costume of the Army of the British Empire" (1812). The Hamilton Smith original actually shows men of the Line and Light battalions and 3rd Hussars of the King's German Legion; but our exercise is perhaps valid, in showing off the details of the light cavalry shabraque in all its glory. This item was not normally seen on campaign.

(**Above & right**) At the end of a day's march or duty away from barracks the hussar had plenty of work to do before he could tend to his own comfort. As soon as the horse was got into stables or bivouac the girth, breastplate and crupper were loosened; the valise, cloak, saddle cover and arms were taken off, as was the bridle. The bits were washed and the stirrup irons wiped clean. Loose litter was then shaken under the horse, and his feet were picked clean. The hussar then took a "wisp" - a good handful of the bedding straw - and gave his horse a rub down, paying attention to its head, ears, underside and legs. After the horse had cooled down sufficiently it was unsaddled, and given fresh hay and hard feed - oats. The hussar was then free to take his valise, cloak and arms to his quarters, where he cleaned his weapons carefully before returning them to the armoury (if in barracks).

These hussars carry only a fraction of the piles of equipment needed to put on an effective cavalry impression. The valise was the cavalryman's equivalent of the infantry knapsack. The hussar's "necessaries" included such things as spare shirt, stockings, foraging cap, stable jacket and duck breeches, a bag for washing and shaving kit, "black ball" (polish) and pipe clay. In the top flap of the valise there was a linen compartment for the currie comb, horse brushes, sponge for the dock (tail) and eyes, mane comb and oil tin. Looking at all these items, reconstructed to exact measurements, it is no small wonder that they could all be crammed into the valise.

(**Left & above**) Impressions of a trumpeter and a private of the 15th Hussars in post-1812 summer campaign dress; during the 1815 Waterloo campaign the regiment was brigaded with the 7th and the 2nd KGL Hussars in Grant's Fifth Brigade. The trumpeter has a bugle, which regimental records confirm that the 15th used during the Corunna campaign. He is otherwise distinguished only by riding a grey, as by 1812 the former practice of dressing cavalry trumpeters in reversed colours - in the 15th, a red uniform faced blue - had been ordered abandoned.

Royal Artillery

The Royal Artillery of the Napoleonic era was a distinctly separate branch of the Army. For historical reasons it was directed not by Horse Guards (roughly the equivalent of today's Ministry of Defence), but by the Master-General of Ordnance, the corps depot and academy being established at Woolwich. It was a small corps, despite a steady expansion during the Napoleonic Wars; and this was partly because of its high standard of training. Artillery officers, like those of the tiny Engineer corps, were the most professional in the Army, and could not purchase promotions. They formed a close-knit family, proud of their technical competence and rather distant from the other officers of the Army. Their corps organisation was also more complex.

The Royal Artillery was composed of battalions, but these were administrative units only; for field service they were dispersed in company-size "brigades". The foot artillery brigade had six pieces of ordnance - usually five 6-pounder (later 9-pounder) guns and one 5^1/$_2$in. howitzer; two captains, three junior officers, four sergeants, four corporals, nine bombardiers, three drummers, and 116 gunners. About 100 men from the then-separate (and much despised) Corps of Drivers were attached to handle the 200-odd draft animals needed to haul the six guns with their limbers and more than a dozen ammunition, baggage, wheel and forge wagons.

The foot battalions also provided the manpower for the garrison artillery mounted in permanent fortifications; and the siege artillery, serving guns of 18- to 24-pound shot weight dragged by teams of 16 oxen, or even massive 32- and 42-pounders. Wellington was never strong in field artillery, but suffered particularly from the lack of a good siege-train.

While all artillery was horse-drawn, the Royal Horse Artillery was a separate and relatively new branch with an elite reputation. The distinction was that while the men of the foot brigades marched with their guns, all gunners of the RHA were mounted or rode on the vehicles. They were trained to march with the cavalry and to manoeuvre fast enough to support them, bringing their pieces smartly into action, and withdrawing with equal speed. Their "troops", also of six pieces, had slightly fewer men and rather more horses than a foot brigade. The troops were organised and trained to operate together, or in two halves, or in three two-gun divisions.

In a battle of position, like Waterloo, the foot brigades and horse troops would fight together, usually dispersed along the line of battle slightly forward of or in the intervals between the bodies of infantry. Each gun crew would have immediately available, with the gun or in its nearby caisson, anything between 100 and 200 rounds - enough for at least two hours' continuous firing at a normal rate of about one shot a minute (which would not in fact be kept up for any great length of time). The dangers gunners faced were counter-battery fire from enemy artillery; the sniping of men and horses by enemy sharpshooters; or

(**Above**) Sergeant-major of the Chatham & Gillingham Artillery Volunteers, the re-enactment group based on Fort Amherst in Kent. The group wear basically RA foot artillery dress of c.1806-1814, though Volunteers like these may have worn only six yellow lace bastion-shaped loops on the red-faced blue jacket, instead of nine. There is a reference to a sergeant-major wearing this version with red lapels buttoned back; many details of period artillery uniform are still rather obscure, being available only from few and sometimes contradictory sources. Note the four gold chevrons, the gold lace, waist sash and swordbelt of his rank.

(**Opposite top left & right**) The officer of the Fort Amherst unit wears everyday uniform of the early years of the 19th century: a large bicorne with a white tuft; an unlaced, long-tailed coat faced red; and legwear of choice - for parades, white breeches and Hessian boots, but otherwise blue pantaloons or blue or grey riding overalls, as here.

(**Right**) The crew serve a 9-pounder gun mounted on a reproduction of a period garrison carriage. The Fort Amherst group have access to a wide range of period guns; there is an ongoing repair and reconstruction programme involving original barrels and reproduction carriages, so the artillery element in the Napoleonic re-enactment scene may hope to grow.

The gunners' uniform of red – faced blue jacket with yellow lace, white breeches and black knee-length gaiters is correct for home service; in the Peninsula they would have worn the same grey campaign trousers and half-gaiters as the infantry.

being overrun by cavalry - and even then, as at Waterloo, crews could often temporarily take cover with the infantry, returning to their guns later. Unless the enemy took the time to dismount and hammer spikes into the touch-holes there was little serious damage they could do to a muzzle-loading cast iron or bronze cannon.

(**Left & below**) A group from the Chester area re-create a Royal Horse Artillery gun crew. They manhandle their 6-pounder into position, recalling a painting by the contemporary artist Dighton: no small task. Even the light RHA version of the 6-pdr. weighed three-quarters of a ton, and the 9-pdr. which had largely replaced it by 1815, a ton and a quarter.

(**Below**) The loading cycle for a muzzle-loading field piece was complex. After a recoil of about six feet the entire crew (four plus the NCO, not counting ammunition carriers) would wrestle it back into position. The spongeman, standing right of the muzzle, wetted the sheepskin sponge end of his staff in the leather water bucket, and swabbed the barrel to douse any smouldering debris. From the left the loader, supplied by one of the four ammunition carriers, then pushed a "fixed round" into the muzzle - a powder charge in a serge bag attached to the ball by a wooden block and tin straps. The ventsman, standing right of the breech, put his thumb (in a leather stall) over the touch-hole or vent to prevent a rush of air fanning any remaining spark into

flame, while the spongeman rammed the charge home with the solid end of his staff. The ventsman then thrust a brass pricker down the vent to pierce the charge bag, inserting a firing tube - a quill filled with powder, forming an instantaneous fuze. The NCO gun captain then laid the piece, adjusting the aim by levering the end of the trail. On his command the firer touched his portfire - a staff fitted with a quickmatch, lit from the linstock with smouldering slowmatch which stood between each pair of guns - to the firing tube. The gun captain watched for the fall of shot; and the sequence began again.

(**Right**) The spongeman with his staff. The RHA uniform kept the basic artillery colours of blue faced with red and laced yellow, but was of a dashing light cavalry style, with a braided dolman jacket. These grey riding overalls with red stripes and deep tan leather cuffing were worn from about 1810; light cavalry sabres were carried; and the bearskin-crested leather "Tarleton" helmet was of the type worn by light dragoons before their uniform changes of 1812.

The 6-pdr. of the re-created RHA crew is an original barrel with a carefully reconstructed carriage and tools. Guns such as this would have fired three types of ammunition: roundshot, canister and spherical case. Roundshot was the simple solid cannonball; with a maximum range of up to 1,500 yards but effective at 600-700 yards, it could tear bloody lanes through formed units of troops. Canister, murderous at short range and effective out to 350-400 yards, was a tin cylinder packed with musket balls; rupturing at the muzzle, it threw them out in a cone-shaped cloud, 32 feet across at 100 yards. Roundshot and canister were often loaded together for close firing. Only the British had spherical case, which immortalised its inventor Lt.Shrapnel. Filled with balls and a bursting charge, and exploded in the air over the target by a time-fuze lit by the discharge of the gun, it was effective between 700 and 1,500 yards.

Following the Drum

A soldier's life in Wellington's day was bleak in respect of domestic comforts. The Army actively discouraged the rank and file from marrying; only six men in every hundred were officially allowed married status, with the commanding officer's permission - this meant that their wives could live with them in barracks and were allowed to draw a soldier's rations.

A married man who tried to keep his family with him after enlisting had no better chance than any other soldier of getting his wife onto the ration strength. Unrecognised wives and sweethearts had to make shift as best they could; there were no restrictions against such relationships, but the soldier was not allowed to live outside barracks. His woman could seek a roof and work nearby; but their prospects were meagre, on pay of a shilling a day before deductions.

When a battalion was posted overseas the recognised wives were allowed to accompany their men, some even taking young children with them; the strict limits on the number allowed on the ration strength led to heartbreaking scenes as the women were drawn by lot at the port of departure. The "lucky" women marched with the battalion's baggage, sharing every hardship and many of the dangers of campaign life.

Today women take an active part in the Napoleonic re-enactment scene, filling many and varied roles. They help bring many a "living history" event to life for the public; the English Heritage "Wellington's Army" displays are fine examples of what can be achieved.

(Below) A "living history" display by members of the re-created 68th Light Infantry at Berwick barracks in Northumberland; this gives an impression of how one of the cheerless barrack rooms of the period might have appeared in use. Typically, 20 men were quartered in a room no more than 32ft.x 20ft. and 7ft. high, where they lived, ate, and slept two (or even four) men to a wooden cot or "crib". If one of the company's half-dozen married couples were allocated to a room, their only privacy was a blanket slung as a curtain; behind it they spent such time as they had together, and here their children were born and raised.

The only light came from candles; sanitation was a bucket; and water came from a pump outside in the yard. Tuberculosis and rheumatism were common. In barracks there was no provision for any kind of recreation; men smoked, drank and gambled in their rooms, or visited nearby taverns and "stews" if they had a few coppers to spend.

If these conditions seem too harsh for anyone to accept for a shilling a day and rations, it should be recalled that they were probably no worse than many poor labourers then endured in civil life, and at least offered security.

(Left) A very convincing portrayal of a soldier's woman. On campaign the rankers' wives made a modest income by taking on chores for their husbands' comrades: they are shown in contemporary prints cooking, laundering and mending in camp.

(Below left) A member of the re-created 95th Rifles in a "living history" camp with his woman. From period memoirs most rankers' wives seem to have been very loyal, making what comfort they could for their husbands under the most primitive conditions. There are pitiable accounts of wives searching battlefields at night for their missing men. If they were widowed on campaign, however, most seem to have remarried without delay in order to stay on the ration strength - there were generally plenty of offers for their hand. Over the course of the Peninsular War some buried a number of husbands one after another.

(Right & below) Army regulations of the period made a blunt distinction between soldiers' "women" and officers' "ladies"; the modern re-enactment scene does not! At the occasional salons and balls held as part of the Napoleonic re-enactment season female members sometimes have the welcome opportunity to exchange campfire and tent for the finery of Regency ladies.

Whatever the subject period, the involvement of female members in basically military groups has many advantages - as foreseen back in the 1960s by Brig.Peter Young, founder of the English Civil War "Sealed Knot Society" and father of British historical re-enactment. Apart from their obvious contributions to the uniforming of their groups, and their frequent administrative help, their presence in costume adds to the public appeal of displays, and is central to the "living history" aspect of the hobby.

(Above & right) Soldiers' women cooking during English Heritage displays. In Napoleonic days the heavy cauldrons and other camping gear would have been carried on the battalion's baggage carts or mules, with which the women marched (often riding donkeys) at the tail of the column under a small escort. Wives were subject to the same code of discipline as their men; accounts mention the difficulties of the provosts in keeping these often formidable women in order.

In general, contemporary writings leave an impressive record of the women's courage and endurance. Their sufferings during hard marches and retreats were dreadful: some perished by the roadside from exhaustion, exposure, illness or accident; some fell behind and were captured, or simply disappeared; many loyally helped their sick or hurt husbands keep up with the column, carrying their packs and muskets. There is an account - by no means unique - from the hideous winter retreat to Corunna, of a pregnant Irish-woman giving birth by the roadside, then calmly wrapping up her baby and continuing the march; mother and child both survived the campaign. Army women seem often to have had one or more infants with them; there must have been many orphans, taken up and cared for by the other women of the camp. (The presence of these children led to some extraordinarily late witnesses of these campaigns: at least two who had been four- and five-year-olds in the camps at Waterloo were still alive in 1903.)

Perhaps more surprising to modern ears are the many records of officers' wives accompanying their husbands on campaign. While comparative wealth made their lives slightly more comfortable, it could not shelter them from cold, exhaustion, sickness or brutal bereavement. Despite their relatively gentler up-bringing most seem to have coped as bravely as the soldier's wives. Wellington's army were not Victorians, and all its men and women were bred in a tougher school than we might imagine.

The EUROPA-MILITARIA Series

Full-colour photographic paperback reference books on the armies of yesterday and today, for collectors, re-enactors, modellers, illustrators, and military history students of all kinds. 64 pages, 260x190mm; UK price £9.95, US price $15.95:

EM No. 1: "Paras - French Paratroops Today"
EM No. 2: "World War II Infantry in Colour Photographs"
EM No. 3: "World War I Infantry in Colour Photographs"
EM No. 4: "Allied Battle Tanks - Central European Frontier"
EM No. 5: "US Marine Corps in Colour Photographs"
EM No. 6: "Waffen-SS Uniforms in Colour Photographs"
EM No. 7: "Operation Desert Shield - The First 90 Days"
EM No. 8: "Air War Over the Gulf"
EM No. 9: "82nd Airborne Division in Colour Photographs"
EM No.10: "The French Foreign Legion Today"
EM No.11: "The French Foreign Legion in Action"
EM No.12: "Military Model Showcase"
EM No.13: "101st Airborne Division in Colour Photographs"
EM No.14: "Red Army Uniforms of WWII in Colour Photographs"
EM No.16: "US Navy SEALs"

EUROPA-MILITARIA SPECIALS
96 pages, UK price £12.95, US price $19.95:

EMS No.1: "The American Civil War
             Recreated in Colour Photographs"

EMS No.2: "The Roman Legions
             Recreated in Colour Photographs"

EMS No.3: "Vietnam: US Uniforms in Colour Photographs"

EMS No.4: "The English Civil War
             Recreated in Colour Photographs"

For further details of our other military, automotive and aviation lists, please contact The Sales Manager, Windrow & Greene Ltd., 19A Floral Street, London WC2E 9DS